20,000 LEAGUES
UNDER THE SEA
OR
DAVID COPPERFIELD

by Robert Benchley

WITH ILLUSTRATIONS BY GLUYAS WILLIAMS

BLUE RIBBON BOOKS
GARDEN CITY, NEW YORK

ACKNOWLEDGMENT

The author wishes to thank the following periodicals for permission to reprint the articles in this book: *The Bookman, The Detroit Athletic Club News, The Forum, Life, The New Yorker,* and *The Yale Review.*

CONTENTS

PAGE

POLITICAL PARTIES AND THEIR GROWTH . . . 3
THE LOW STATE OF WHIPPET RACING . . . 7
ADD FOLK PLAYS 16
MEETING THE BOATS 23
"IN THIS CORNER—" 33
'ROUND AND 'ROUND AND 'ROUND 40
THE COOPER CYCLE IN AMERICAN FOLK SONGS . 45
HOCKEY TONIGHT! 49
"I AM IN THE BOOK" 56
A SHORT HISTORY OF AMERICAN POLITICS . . 66
THE BRIDGE OF SANS GENE 70
TRY-OUTS 77
AFRICAN SCULPTURE 83
FOOTBALL SAGAS 89
MR. MENCKEN REVIEWS MR. NATHAN AND VICE
  VERSA 95
CLINICAL NOTES 98
THE NEW SOCIAL BLIGHT 101
PASSPORT DOPE 108
"ISLAND IRISH." 110
ON THE AIR 116
FASCINATING CRIMES 126
THE PROBLEM OF THE USED CAR 131
CHECKING UP 134
A SHORT (WHAT THERE IS OF IT) HISTORY OF
  AMERICAN POLITICAL PROBLEMS 138

PAGE

CEASE FIRING! 142

THE GREAT AMERICAN FOLLY 148

JUNIOR DRAMA 156

THE PASSING OF THE COW 161

BACK TO THE GAME 166

IT SEEMS THERE WERE A COUPLE OF CELLS . . 176

NO RESULTS WHATEVER IN OUR OWN STRAW VOTE 178

TWO EDITORIALS FOR "THE NATION" . . . 182

MR. KELLOGG'S DILEMMA 184

THE FOUR-IN-HAND OUTRAGE 185

SIGNIFICANT RESULTS IN SECOND WEEK OF OUR OWN STRAW VOTE 190

THE PACKER'S ASSISTANT 193

THE BIRTH OF A COLLEGE COMIC PAPER . . 198

A CHRISTMAS GARLAND OF BOOKS . . . 202

THE WOOLEN MITTEN SITUATION . . . 212

THE TYPICAL NEW YORKER 220

20,000 LEAGUES UNDER THE SEA
OR DAVID COPPERFIELD

POLITICAL PARTIES AND THEIR GROWTH

1. *Introductory Essay*

IT was Taine (of "Taine Goin' to Rain No More") who said: "Democracies defeat themselves." Perhaps I haven't got that quotation right. It doesn't seem to mean much.

However, my point—and I am sure Taine's point, if he were here to make it—is that under the system of government known as a democracy, or, as it is sometimes known, the *Laissez-Faire* system (1745-1810), the ratio of increase in the population will eventually outstrip the ratio of increase in wheat production and then where will we be? Although this theory is generally credited to Malthus, I am not sure that I didn't state it before him. I certainly remember saying it when I was very young.

In writing a history of the political parties of the United States (to which this is the introductory essay and possibly the last chapter as well) one must bear constantly in mind the fact that there are two separate and distinct parties, the Republicans (a clever combination of two Latin words, *res* and *publicæ,* meaning "things of the public") and the Democrats (from the Greek *demos,* meaning something which I will look up before this goes to the printer's). The trick comes in telling which is which.

During the early years of our political history the Republican Party was the Democratic Party, or, if you chose, the Democratic Party was the Republican Party. This led naturally to a lot of confusion, especially in the Democratic Party's getting the Republican Party's mail; so it was decided to call the Republicans "Democrats" and be done with it. The Federalist Party (then located at what is now the corner of Broad and Walnut streets and known as "The Swedish Nightingale") became, through the process of Natural Selection and a gradual dropping-off of its rudimentary tail, the Republican Party as we know it today. This makes, as prophesied earlier in this article, *two* parties, the Republicans and the Democrats. As a general rule, Republicans are more blonde than Democrats.

Now that we have cleared up the matter of the early confusion in names, it remains for us simply to trace the growth of the party platforms from their original sources to their present-day clearly defined and characteristic chaos. This will involve quite a bit of very dull statistical matter and talk about Inflation and Nullification, which will be enlivened by comical stories and snatches of current songs of the period. In fact, talk about Inflation and Nullification may be omitted entirely. It will also be necessary to note the rise and fall of the minor political parties, such as the Free Soil Party, the Mugwumps, the St. Louis Cardinals and Tom ("Rum-Romanism-and-Rebellion") Heflin. This will not be much fun either. As a matter of fact, in outlining the subject matter of this history the thought has come to me that it shapes up as a pretty dry book and I am wondering if perhaps I haven't made a mistake in undertaking it. . . . Oh, well, we'll see.

In compiling these data and writing the book I have been aided immeasurably by the following colleagues, to whom I take this opportunity of expressing my warmest thanks (the warmest thanks on a February 9th since 1906, according to the Weather Bureau atop the Whitehall Building): B. S. Aal, Raymond Aalbue, Aalders Bros., A. C. Aalholm, Alex Aarons, the Aar-Jay Bed-Light Co., Henry W. Aarts, Theo. T. Aarup, Charles Aba, M. M. Abajian, B. Abadessa (Miss), Abbamonte & Frinchini (shoe reprng.) and Lewis Browne Zzyd.

I also wish to thank Dr. Hartmann Weydig for the loan of his interesting collection of shells, with-

out which I would have had nothing to do when I
was not writing the book.

THE AUTHOR.

BIBLIOGRAPHY

"Political Parties and Their Growth, with a Key to
the Calories." Robert Benchley. (Life Pub. Co.)

"Ivanhoe." Sir Walter Scott. (Ginn & Co.)

"Fifty Cocktail Recipes, with Directions for Swallow-
ing." A. M. Herz. (Doubleday-Doran-Doubleday-
Doran-Doubleday-Doran-Boom!)

"An Old-Fashioned Girl." Louisa M. Alcott. (Vir
Pub. Co.)

And countless back-numbers of *Harper's Round Table*.

THE LOW STATE OF WHIPPET RACING

IT does not seem too soon now to begin for-
mulating plans for next year's whippet racing.
While there are still a few more races on the 1928
schedule, most of the important ones have been run
off and the leading whippets have practically all
broken training.

Whippet racing in recent years has deteriorated
into a sordid spectacle, productive of only gigantic
gate receipts for the promoters. At one whippet
race on Long Island last summer, it is estimated
that forty people lined the course, and, as each of
these forty paid something in the neighborhood of
a quarter for parking their cars in a nearby field, it
will be seen that the thing has already got out of
hand and is now in the class of mad sport carnivals.

This has naturally had its reaction on the whippets themselves. They have become mercenary and
callous. All they think of is money, money, money.
The idea of sport for sport's sake is a dream of the
past as far as whippets are concerned. In order to
make the game what it used to be, we shall have to
bring up a whole new breed of whippets and send
the present success-crazed organization out on the

road in circuses where they may indulge their lust for gain without hindrance of any considerations of sportsmanship.

Perhaps a few examples may serve to illustrate my point. I witnessed a whippet race in California recently at which the gate happened to be very small. There had been no publicity worthy of the name and the word had simply got around among the racetrack gang that some whippets were going to race at three o'clock. This brought out a crowd of perhaps six people, exclusive of the owners and trainers. Four of the six were chance passers-by and the other two were state policemen.

Now evidently the small size of the crowd enraged the whippets or, at any rate, threw them into such a state of mind that they gave up all idea of racing and took to kidding. In the first race they were not halfway down the lanes when two of them stopped and walked back, while the other two began wrestling good-naturedly. The owners at the finish line called frantically, but to no avail, and the race had to be called off.

In the second race they would not even start. When the gun was fired, they turned as if by pre-arranged mutiny and began jumping up and kissing their trainers. This race also had to be called off.

By this time the crowd was in an ugly humor.

By this time the crowd was in an ugly humor and one or two started to boo. The state police, scenting trouble, went home. This left four spectators and further upset the whippets. A conference of the owners and trainers resulted in what you might call practically nothing. It got along toward supper time and even I went home. I looked in the papers the next morning but could find no news of the races, so I gathered that the rest of the heats had been called off too.

This pretty well indicates the state in which whippet racing now finds itself in this country. The remedy is up to those of us old whippet fanciers who have the time and the means to reform the thing from the ground up.

First, I would recommend a revision of the system of whippet-calling. As you no doubt know, a whippet race is at least one-third dependent on calling. The trainer leads the whippet from the finish line up the lane to the starting point (a silly procedure to begin with) and then holds him in leash until the gun. The owner, or some close personal friend, stands at the finish line and calls to the whippet, which is supposed to drive him crazy and make him run like mad back down the lane again in a desire to reach his owner. As we have seen, the whippet can take it or leave it and is by no means certain to show any desire at all to get back to the caller. Now this must be due to the calling. If the thing were made attractive at all for the whippet to reach the finish line, we would see no more of this hopping up and kissing trainers at the start.

As near as I could distinguish, most of the owners called out, "Come on, Luke!" or "Here, Bennie, here!" Now obviously there was nothing very exciting about these calls. You or I wouldn't run like mad down a lane to get to someone who was calling, "Come on, Charlie!" or "Here, Bob, here!" (unless, of course, it was Greta Garbo who was doing the calling. In that case, a short, sharp whistle would be O.K.)

There must be some more attractive sounds made to entice the whippets down the lanes. Not knowing exactly what it is that whippets like best, it is a little difficult for me to make suggestions. I don't know and I don't pretend to know. All I am sure of is that the whippets aren't particularly attracted by what is being held out to them now.

Now in the matter of blankets. On the way up the lanes to the starting point, the whippets are forced to wear blankets like race horses. This saps not only their vitality but their self-respect. It is all right for a race horse to wear a blanket if he wants to, because he is big and can carry it off well.   But when you get a whippet who, even with everything showing, can hardly be seen unless you have him in your lap, and then cover him up in a

It just makes a nance out of him.

blanket, it just makes a nance out of him, that's all. They look like so many trotting blankets, and they must know it.   A whippet has feelings as well as the rest of us.   You can't make a dog ashamed to appear in public and then expect him to run a race.   If they have to be kept warm, give each one a man's-size shot of rye before he starts up the course. You'd get better racing that way, too. With a good hooker of rye inside him, a whippet might not really be running fast but he would

The owner or some close personal friend stands at the finish line and calls to the whippet.

think that he was, and that's something. As it stands, they are so ashamed of their blankets that they have to do something on the way down the lanes to appear virile. So they stop right in the middle of the race and wrestle.

This wrestling business calls for attention, too. It is all right for dogs to kid, but they don't have to do it in the middle of a race. It is as if Charlie Paddock, while running the hundred, should stop after about fifty yards and push one of his opponents playfully on the shoulder and say, "Last tag!" and then as if his opponent should stop and chase Charlie around in the track trying to tag him back. What kind of time would they make in a race like that?

I don't think that the thing has ever been put up to the whippets quite frankly in this manner. If someone could take a few whippets to a track meet and (the whole gag having been worked up before, of course, among the runners) the thing should deteriorate into a rough-and-tumble clowning match of pushing and hauling one another, the whippets might see what it looks like. You could say to them: "Now you see, that's how *you* look when you stop in the middle of a race and wrestle all over the track." They would be pretty ashamed, I should think.

The less said about their jumping up and kissing their trainers at the start, the better. This is something that a good psychoanalyst ought to handle. But so long as it is allowed to go on, whippet racing will be in the doldrums. And so

long as whippet racing is in the doldrums—well,
it is in the doldrums, that's all.

Better in the doldrums, say I, than for the whippets to so far forget the principles of good, clean
amateur sport as to pursue a mechanical rabbit.

ADD FOLK PLAYS

THE past few weeks have belonged to the amateur rather than to the professional in what, for lack of a longer term, we will call Our National Theatre.

Broadway may have been dark, but our schools and colleges have been a-buzz with exclamations of parental pride mingled with the murmurings of the prompter, as the actors and actresses of the Little Theatre of To-morrow creaked back and forth across the temporary stages and made believe they were somebody else.

These performances have ranged in ambition from outdoor Greek drama (at times a bit hurried in tempo because of the rumbled threat of a shower in the offing) to class-reunion shows "worked up" late in the afternoon before the performance. Of the two, the latter type is easier to watch.

In these informal productions there is less strain on the actors, whose only concern is to keep upright and *on* the stage. And, as in any theatrical performance, professional or otherwise, the less strain there is on the actors, the easier it is for the audience.

16

Entrance of a fair proportion of the cast, in reunion costume.

Although these strange folk-plays performed at class reunions appear in no manuscript form to speak of, a transcript of the proceedings (taken down by a broad-minded male stenographer) might read, in part, as follows:

ACT 2

(Act 1 having been omitted owing to the non-appearance of five of the principals. These appear somewhat later and insist on giving their act on the veranda while Act 2 is still in progress. Their audience is recruited in large blocs from the main auditorium.)

Entrance of a fair proportion of the cast, in reunion costume, with some attempt at rhythmic movement to the tune of "Hallelujah"! The lyric, as picked out by watching the lips of the more capable singers, seems to be:

"Hallelu-jah! Hallelu-jah! Here we are, Big 1912.
(Repeat)
Nobody something something something,
But you can't something, something, something,
Hallelu-jah! Hallelu-jah! Here we are, Big 1912!"

Apparent end of song, although several die-hards continue for another line or two, amid thunderous applause. A conference of principals is then held and it is decided to give in to the popular demand and sing the whole number again, with repeats. At the conclusion of this, in spite of vociferous demands from sections of the audience for more, the dialogue is launched:

1ST CITIZEN: Well, well, what ever became of George Wisser?

VOICE FROM AUDIENCE: Yeah! Wisser!

2ND VOICE FROM AUDIENCE: He went to Princeton!

ENTIRE AUDIENCE: Yeah—Princeton!

1ST CITIZEN (*addressing audience personally*): He couldn't go to Princeton, he didn't have a signet ring. (*Entirely extemporaneous line but very popular.*)

2ND CITIZEN (*with some idea of getting along with the show*): Well, Eddie, what *did* become of George Wisser?

GEORGE WISSER (*from audience*): Here I am! Fast asleep!

(*At this, pandemonium breaks loose, and, encouraged by cries of "We want Wisser!" Mr. Wisser climbs up on the stage and joins the cast.*)

3RD CITIZEN: Why, hello, George! Want to be in the show?

GEORGE WISSER (*suddenly disgusted with the*

"Here I am! Fast asleep!"

whole thing): No! (*Climbs down and goes back to his seat.*)

At this point some one, dressed for no reason at all to represent President Lowell of Harvard, arises and announces that there will now be a song by Arthur Welson entitled: "If I Send My Son to the Dental School, Will a Gold-Digger Teach the Class?" This is met by a storm of disapproval, and Arthur Welson is never heard, chiefly because of cries of "Louder!"

At this point the entire entertainment is taken over by the audience for a period of about ten minutes. Six or seven members climb up on the stage and three or four of the cast visit with cronies in the audience. "Hallelujah!" is sung several times and one or two announcements are made, preceded by much banging for order.

Finally, one of the class marshals makes himself heard to the following extent:

CLASS MARSHAL: Come on, now, fellows! Tony and the rest have worked hard on this show and are trying to do something for the class. The least we can do is to sit still and be quiet. Everybody back in his seat, now!

There is general cheering at this and several of the more earnest classmates take their seats. The rest mill about at random.   In the meantime, the show has been begun again, starting with the entrance of the chorus singing "Hallelujah!"

This goes on for some time.

CURTAIN

MEETING THE BOATS

ONE of the worst phases of staying in America all summer is what is known as "meeting the boats." By this is meant going down to the docks to welcome incoming travelers. It is an incredibly cruel rite and should be abolished.

In the first place, the boat-meeter has presumably been stewing in New York for at least three days before the boat is due—sometimes all summer. He is in no mood to meet anything—much less a boatful of buoyant vacationists. Even if it were possible for him just to go downstairs in his hotel and have the boat dock right in the lobby, he wouldn't be any too game. But docking in a hotel lobby is something they haven't worked up yet, modern science or no modern science. At present, it is the invariable rule of steamers to find out where you (the meeters) are and then to dock at a point as inacessible as the topography of New York will permit. And the topography of New York permits almost anything.

It is always well to call up the office of the steamship company the day before the boat is due and

23

ask at what hour she will dock. You will talk with some very small child who seems to be dazed by your question and who gives you an answer which is palpably wrong, provided it will parse at all. This will put you on your guard. You will then see that you are up against no ordinary emergency and will begin to worry. All this helps the general effect and makes the day more unpleasant.

There are two possibilities for the next day. One is that you will arrive at the dock (a) too early and (b) too late. The records show no instance of anyone's arriving just as the gangplank was put down. This would be contrary to maritime law.

Arriving too early is much the worse method of procedure, which is probably what makes so many people arrive late. When you arrive early there is grave danger of going insane while waiting. A rumor that the boat is due at 9 A.M. brings you sweating to the pier at 9:10. You dash up the dock and see a boat already being unloaded and most of its passengers gone. This is terrifying. A wild seach among the remaining battlers with the customs officers reveals no familiar face. Inquiries of stewards, if it is a non-English-speaking crew (and it always is), get you nothing but pleasant nods and queer noises. Just as you are about to leave the dock in a panic, you see the name of the ship on

A wild search reveals no familiar face.

her bow. It is *not* the ship you are meeting. Your ship is due on the other side of the pier.

And then begins the long vigil. An official says that she is in Quarantine and will dock in half an hour. Another says she will be in in ten minutes. Another says she hasn't left Cherbourg yet. So you decide not to leave and go back to bed as you would like to do but to stick it out. Half an hour isn't bad. It isn't good, either.

Now half an hour—an hour—two hours—on a North River pier with nothing to do is what makes radicals of people. No matter what the weather may be out in the street, on the pier it is damp and cold. There is a preparation in the construction of piers which is calculated to eat through shoe soles in twenty minutes and freeze feet in forty-five. This gets in its work the minute you put foot on the dock.

The question of entertainment while you are waiting is a knotty one. You may run very fast up and down the pier until you are exhausted and fall unconscious. If unconsciousness is your aim, however, there are less nervous ways of acquiring it, although the use of stimulants to this end is to be deplored, as it is likely to result in nasty complications with dock officials and your being put off entirely. A slow, carefully nursed bun might work

out well, but it is very hard to gauge those things.
You think you are nursing it along carefully and

Why don't they dock ships in hotel lobbies?

the next thing you know you are over on your face
with an ugly gash in your forehead.

There are games that the waiter can play among
the boxes and crates on a pier provided he likes
games, but, if you happen to be all alone, it is rather
difficult not to look silly playing them. One of the

least suspicious-looking games for the lone waiter to play is counting all the crates and seeing if he can give each one the name of a prominent character in history.

It is unwise to keep asking officials when the boat is going to dock, as they know no more about it than you do and it just irritates them. On the other hand, it is well to keep in friendly contact with some one of the pier authorities, otherwise they will think that you are a Red, snooping about to blow up the dock. Either way, you are going to make yourself unpopular. Either way, you are going to catch cold.

Now, let us suppose for the sake of argument that the ship finally docks. You are standing in the crowd at the foot of the gangplank, trying to spot your mother or your wife or whatever it is you are meeting. After a few abortive waves at the wrong people, you decide that a sense of dignity alone requires you to keep your gestures under control; so you stand impassive until practically all the passengers are off. Then you begin to wonder. Has there been a burial at sea? Has your loved one fallen into the machinery? Whoever the people are that get off boats first, they are never by any chance *your* people. They must be *somebody's* people, because somebody is there to meet them. But *your* people are always the last to get off a train, a boat, or out of a theatre or football stadium. That's the way life is.

Let us again suppose, for the sake of argument (if anybody cares to argue), that they finally appear, all very flustered and in somewhat of a daze. You rather expect to have them impressed at the sacrifice of time and money that you have made to be down at the pier to greet them, but no. This is taken for granted. Of course, your mother or your wife you *have* to be down at the pier to meet, but you *certainly* don't have to go out of your way to meet anybody else, and the next time they can just meet themselves and see how they like it.

Your presence is not only taken for granted but also your contribution toward the customs duties. "Oh, *have* you got fifty dollars with you, Bob?" they say; "we haven't had our money changed yet and this man says that I have to pay excess on my coat." So out comes the fifty dollars (if you are sap enough to have it on you) and away it goes into the coffers of the United States Customs House—zip! You can also take care of the bags and get them into a cab and you can see that the porters are taken care of and that the steward (who has been so awfully nice) gets a little something extra for coming 'way out to the stairs with you.

I went to meet Donald Ogden Stewart (I men-

tion no names) and bride on their return from their
honeymoon. They landed in Hoboken, necessitat-
ing my leaving New York before daylight. Well,
it seems that they had plans to go to Princeton to
the Yale-Princeton game that afternoon, and, as it
would be so much easier for them to drive right
from the pier in Hoboken to Princeton, it was only
logical that old Bob should take the bags (nineteen
pieces) and little Lucy (the worst dog ever smug-
gled into America) over to New York for them and
get them a room at a hotel—a hotel where one could
keep dogs.

I didn't want to do this—and did it with very
bad grace—but nevertheless I found myself in a
cab with nineteen pieces of baggage (including
Lucy's dog-house) *and* Lucy, bound for Manhattan.
That was a Saturday noon.

Late Sunday afternoon we were found on the
beach at Yaphank, Long Island. There were only
five pieces of baggage left, and I had eaten part of
Lucy while Lucy had eaten part of me. I remember nothing after visiting the eighth hotel and being
told that one could not bring dogs in. The Stew-
arts tell me that they had a swell time at Princeton
and that I ought to have gone.

This was the last boat that I met until I had
to meet my wife this spring. I determined not to

Whoever the people are that get off boats first, they are never by any chance your people.

get there too early and consequently tore up just as the last passengers were leaving the pier. I had forgotten to get a dock permit and was forced to scream over the top of a picket fence at my wife and two little boys who were standing huddled under the "B" sign, crying softly and on the verge of being taken up by the Travelers' Aid Society.

My wife beckoned for me to come over.

"I can't!" I replied. "I have trachoma."

At this my entire family burst into tears and got back on the boat to return to France. I couldn't get in touch with them until I had been to the American consul's and got a photograph of myself with two sides to it, one for the government and one for the class-book. Even then they were pretty cross at me.

So I have given up meeting boats. You can't win. The best way is to go abroad yourself and get met.

"IN THIS CORNER—"

FRANKLY, I am not much of a fight fan. I always get sorry for the one who is getting socked. On the other hand, if *no* one is getting socked, I am bored and start screaming for blood. There is no such thing as pleasing me at a fight.

Of course, as I keep saying to myself when I get to worrying over the loser's suffering, he probably expects this sort of thing. When a man decides to be a fighter he must know that sooner or later he is going to get his nose mashed in. He takes that chance. So there is really no need for me to feel so bad about it. God knows, I have troubles enough of my own without sitting and wincing every time some Lithuanian bunker-boy gets punched in the side of the head.

But somehow I can't help feeling that the one who is getting mashed is pretty fairly surprised that things have taken this turn—and not a little mortified. I am afraid that he didn't want to fight in the first place, but was forced into it by his backers. Perhaps, if I read more of the fighters' statements before the fight, I would feel a little less sorry for them when I hear their faces give way. Once I

33

read what a welterweight said on the day before the contest, and, for the first time, I actually enjoyed seeing his lip swell up.

Probably my tender feelings in the matter are due to an instinctive habit I have of putting myself in the place of anyone I am watching. I haven't been at a fight for more than three minutes before I begin indulging in one of my favorite nightmares. This consists of imagining that I myself am up in the ring facing the better of the two men.

Just how I am supposed to have got up in the ring is never quite clear. I don't believe that I ever would sign up deliberately for a prize fight, much as I need the money. I can think of at least fourteen thousand things that I would try first. But the idea seems to be that while drugged or under the influence of alcohol I have agreed to meet some prominent pugilist in the Yankee Stadium and, quite naturally, the affair has filled the mammoth bowl with a record crowd, all of whom are cynically antagonistic to me.

Whatever my mental processes may have been which led me to don silken tights and crawl through the ropes, my reverie begins when I awake to find myself standing under the terrific glare of the lights going through the formality of shaking gloves with a very large man.

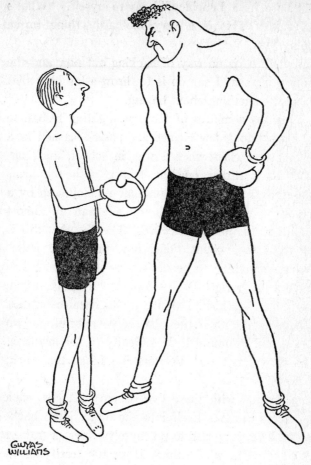

"Here, here, Benchley," I say to myself. "This is a very
foolhardy thing to be doing."

"Here, here, Benchley," I say to myself. "What's all this? This is a very foolhardy thing to be doing."

But there is no way of backing out now and the only thing that I can do is to throw a big bluff that I know something about boxing.

Now, as a matter of fact, my fighting technique is limited to a few elementary passes learned in a gymnasium class when I was in school, and consists of a rather trusting stance with the arms raised as if posing for a photograph, followed by a quick lunge forward with my left and an almost simultaneous jump backward. The fact that this is all done to a count, "one, two, three, and four," leaves something to be desired as strategy. I also have a nasty right hook—done to "five, six, seven, and eight"—which, I think, would deceive no one. I have tried both of these on the younger of my two boys, and he found little difficulty in solving them the very first time. Fortunately, I had the reach, however.

Equipped with these two primary attacks, each of which resolves itself into the quick jump backward, I am supposed to pit myself against a trained fighter. The whole thing is pretty terrifying to start with and rapidly grows worse.

The trouble with my position No. 1 seems to be

that my opponent doesn't wait for me. No sooner have I taken my stance and raised my fists than I am the recipient of a terrific clout on the ear, without even the formality of counting "one, two, three, and four." Without seeing very much of anything at the time, I try my left hook, which ends very badly somewhere in midair, and again take a rapid succession of neck-bending socks on either side of the jaw. At this juncture, I decide to lie down.

This strategy on my part is greeted with derisive hoots from the crowd, but there seems to be nothing else to be done about it. There is practically nothing that my opponent can't do to me and nobody knows it better than I do. Furthermore, I am not one of those people who develop a gameness under physical pain. I am not a glutton for punishment. If I had my way about it I would practically *never* let myself be hurt. In the waiting room of a dentist's office I have been known to develop a yellow streak which is clearly visible through my clothing. Gameness is a grand quality and it is all right as a last resort, but my motto is "Try everything else first."

Consequently, in the position in which I now find myself, my first thought is how to get out of the ring and into bed with the covers pulled over my head. I try crawling out through the ropes, but in this particular dream-fight of mine, there is a rule against throwing in the towel. Both fighters must go the entire fifteen rounds, dead or alive. So you can see my predicament.

I very seldom get much farther than this point in my reverie. I suppose that I would just lie there on the floor and make my opponent come to me if he wanted to hit me. I am very certain that I would not be fool enough to get up on my feet again. I might try kicking him in the shins from my recumbent position, but I doubt that I would bring myself to even that show of belligerence. I would simply have to trust in his seeing the humor of the thing and good-naturedly getting down on the floor beside me and wrestling the rest of the fight out. He would win that, too, but I wouldn't get those socks on the side of the head at any rate.

As I snap out of this dream state and find myself sitting in my safe ringside seat (from which I can see nothing, owing to the holders of ringside seats in front of me indulging in the good American custom of standing up whenever things get interesting) my first sensation is one of great relief at my good fortune in not being in the ring. But then I see some other poor son-of-a-gun getting what I might have had, and I can't help but wish that the whole thing would stop. Maybe he, too, found himself up there quite by accident.

Of course, there is one thing about prize fights that one sees nowadays. In a large majority of them no one gets hurt enough even to *want* to stop before it is over. Sometimes it is hard to tell who is the winner, and the most serious injury sustained by either fighter is a little skin rubbed off the inside of his arms from waltzing. At least, I have the distinction of having taken part in the most brutal fight of modern times.

'ROUND AND 'ROUND AND 'ROUND

IN a feverish attempt to make a hundred percent survey of the entertainment facilities of New York City, I have finally gone into the skating-rink situation. My report is, in the main, unfavorable.

Skating is, or should be, a ritualistic procedure. You don't just go out and move your feet along ice. The act itself should be preceded by what is known as "bundling up" (not to be confused with the old New England custom of "bundling"). This should come as the result of a state of mind—the Will to Suffer. There must be a definite masochistic desire on the part of the skater to be uncomfortable. He must court the pain of strapping on skates with chapped and benumbed fingers (although, of course, your modern smart-aleck skater has his skates already attached to his shoes when he leaves home, avoiding the necessity of skating along the brick pavements on his way to the ice by carrying both shoes and skates in his hand and wearing another pair of shoes, thereby complicating the process to the point of almost complete confusion and chaos). And there must also be the ever-present danger of skating into a portion of the pond where there is no ice-formation, resulting in at least a wet leg and possibly complete drowning.

The New York skater who hies himself to an indoor skating-rink like "Iceland" goes through none of this preliminary mental state. He simply says to himself (or, as seems to be the case at "Iceland," *her*self), "I think I will get on some glazed surface and push myself around it for a while and then come back home." So he takes his skates and gets into the subway or a taxi-cab, gets out at Fifty-second Street next to the Theater Guild, pays his money and goes inside to where hundreds of other unimaginative people are going 'round and 'round and 'round in brutish comfort and complete safety, and, when he has completed as many rounds himself as his craving demands, he gets back into the subway and goes home. An effete civilization, if ever I saw one!

When I say that the "Iceland" skaters are making their circuit in complete safety, I neglect one phase of the sport which the indifferent skater would do well to bear in mind. There is always the chance that he will fall down and be cut into shreds by the oncoming hordes behind him. He must keep his feet and his pace, otherwise he will suffer the fate of those primeval mammals who, lacking sufficient

protective coloration or long enough tails, were elim-
inated by their more fortunate mates in the inexor-
able process of Natural Selection. But, aside from
this risk (which, after all, every one of us runs in
his daily existence) skating at "Iceland" is as dull
and colorless as taking the dog out for an airing.

Which brings us quite logically to that even
duller merry-go-round entertainment of mid-winter
New York, the Six Day Bicycle Race. The difference between this mammoth Carnival of Routine
and indoor-rink skating is that you have to watch
it instead of taking part. For one solid week sport-
lovers crowd into Madison Square Garden and sit,
dozing off and knitting, while fifteen or twenty un-
healthy-looking men pedal their way in a mass
around a track to the accompaniment of music from
one of the worst bands outside of Germany. Now
and then terrific excitement reigns when someone
in the audience, out of sheer boredom, offers twenty-
five or a hundred dollars for the winner of a mile
sprint, at the announcement of which the anemic
athletes whip themselves into a faster pace until
they have gone a mile. During the sprints, especially when the riders are on the turns and at an
angle of forty-five degrees, there *is* a certain thrill
if you are seeing it for the first time or even the
second, but as the sleepy spectators are constantly

offering prizes to keep themselves awake, even the sprints become routine after a while and the only excitement comes from watching the alternate riders, who are resting in their Pullman berths at the trackside, as they eat and have their thighs slapped.

As in indoor-skating there is always the danger that one rider will spill, thereby upsetting the entire mob who follow close at his heels, but this happens all too seldom. Subconsciously this must be what the Roman crowd is waiting for, otherwise they would not sit up so late.

There is one feature of the Six Day Bicycle Race which does not obtain in "Iceland" and that is the presence of the Social Set. Along about two-thirty in the morning parties of ladies and gentlemen in evening dress enter, to the accompaniment of hoots and jeers from the plebs, and seat themselves in the boxes to watch the sprints which are scheduled for that hour. Facing them, in the enclosure in the center of the arena and above them in the galleries, are probably all the gorillas and gun-men in New York, for whom the Six Day Race has had a fascination ever since the old Madison Square Garden Days when the gangs used to gather for their annual elimination festival resulting in anywhere from six to eight deaths. On no other occasion in our democratic procedure as a social organization do the forces of unrest and revolt come face to face with their quarries in such numbers or in such a bright light. Some year, when things have gone a little farther, the Six Day Bicycle Race may be the scene of the Great Upheaval and the Garden, in future years, may be known as the Tuileries of America. It is hardly worth going, year after year, to wait for, however. We can read about it in the papers next day just as well.

THE COOPER CYCLE IN AMERICAN FOLK SONGS

A STUDY of the folk-songs of—and indigenous to—the Ohio River Valley (and just a teeny-weeny section of Illinois) discloses the fact that, between 1840 and half-past nine, coopering was the heroic occupation and coopers the legendary heroes of local song and story.

On all sides we come across fragments of ballads, or even the ballads themselves, dealing with the romantic deeds of such characters as *Cris the Cooper,* or *Warburton the Barrel-Maker,* with an occasional reference to *William W. Ransome,* although there is no record of *Ransome's* having been a cooper.

The style in which these cooper-ballads were written would indicate that they were all written by members of the same family, possibly the Jukes. There is the same curious, stilted rhyme-scheme, more like a random idea than a scheme, and a mannerism of harmony which indicates clearly that they were composed on a comb.

Probably the most famous of all these ballads in

praise of coopering is the one called "Ernie Henkle,"
which begins as follows:

> "Oh, my name is Ernie Henkle,
>   Oh, in Rister I was born,
>   Oh, I never let up with my coopering
>   Oh, till I get my rintle on."

(A rintle was the special kind of thumb-piece that
coopers used to thumb down the hoops, before the
invention of the automatic hooper.)

> "Oh, one day 'twas down in Georgia,
>   And that I won't deny,
>   That I met a gal named Sadie Fried,
>   And—(*line lost*)

> "Oh, she stole my heart completely,
>   And that I can't deny,
>   And it wasn't the tenth of August
>   Or the eighteenth of July."

(Here the singer interjects a whistling solo.)

> "When up stepped Theodore Munson,
>   And unto me did say,
>   'Oh, you can't go back on your promised word,'
>   And unto me did say.

> "Oh, I killed that Theodore Munson,
>   And unto him did say,
>   'Oh, the only gal is Henrietta Bascome,
>   And that you can't deny.' "

This goes on for thirty-seven verses and then begins over again and goes over the entire thirty-seven for the second time. By this time every one is pretty sick of it.

But there we see the cooper-ballad at its best. (If you don't believe it, you ought to hear some of the others.) *Ernie Henkle* came to stand for the heroic cooper and, even in later songs about baggage-men, we find the *Henkle* motif creeping in—and out again.

For example, in the famous song about "Joe McGee, the Baggage-Man":

> " 'Twas in the gay December,
>   And the snow was up to your knees,
> When Number 34 pulled 'round the bend
>   As pretty as you please.
> Lord, Lord. As pretty as you please.

> "Now Joe McGee was the baggage man,
>   On Number 34,
> And he sat right down on the engine step
>   And killed that Sam Basinette."

(There seems to be some confusion here as to just *what* Sam Basinette is meant. He must have been referred to in an earlier verse which has been lost.)

> "Now Sam Basinette said before he died,
>   'This ain't no treat to me,

> For the only gal is Henrietta Bascome,
> And that you will agree.' "

It seems that *Henrietta Bascome* was more or less of a prom-girl who rotated between the coopers and the baggage-men in their social affairs, and even got as far north as Minnesota when the roads were clear.

It will be seen that in all these folk-songs the picaresque element is almost entirely lacking: that is, there is very little—perhaps I mean "picturesque" instead of "picaresque." In all these songs the *picturesque* element is lacking; that is, there is very little color, very little movement, very little gin, please. The natives of this district were mostly rude people—constantly bumping into each other and never apologizing—and it is quite likely that they thought these to be pretty good songs, as songs go. That they aren't, is no fault of mine. You ought to know better than to read an article on American folk-songs.

HOCKEY TONIGHT!

THE growth of hockey in the brief period which spans my own life is a matter of great interest to me. Sometimes I sit and think about it for hours at a time. "How hockey has grown!"

"I was never very good at it."

I muse, "How hockey has grown!" And then it is dinnertime and I have done no work.

But, frankly, hockey is a great big sport now, and I can remember when its only function was to humiliate me personally. I never was very good at it, owing to weak ankles which bent at right angles whenever I started out to skate fast after the puck. I was all right standing still or gliding slowly along, but let me make a spurt and—bendo—out they would go! This made me more or less the butt of the game and I finally gave the whole thing up and took to drinking.

But, at that time, hockey was an informal game, played mostly by small boys with a view to hogging the ice when others, including little girls and myself, wanted to skate. It is true, there was a sort of professional hockey played on an indoor rink at Mechanics' Hall, but that was done on roller skates and was called "polo."

"Polo," as played by the professional teams from Fall River and Providence, was the forerunner of the more intimate maneuvers of the Great War. The players were all state charges out on probation, large men who had given their lives over to some form of violence or other, and the idea was to catch the opposing player with the polo stick as near to the temple as possible and so end the game sooner. A good, livid welt across the cheek was considered a compromise, but counted the striker three points, nevertheless, just to encourage marksmanship. It was estimated that the life of an average indoor polo-player was anywhere from six to eight hours.

Then, gradually, the game of ice-hockey came into ascendancy in the colleges. It was made a major sport in many of them, the players winning their letter for playing in the big games and falling behind in their studies, just as in football and baseball. I was on the student council in my own university when the decision was made to give the members of the hockey team a straight letter without the humiliation of crossed hockey sticks as a bar-sinister as heretofore, and the strain of the debate and momentousness of the question were so great that, after it had all been decided and the letters had been awarded, we all had to go and lie down and rest. Some of us didn't get up again for four or five days. I sometimes wonder if I *ever* got up.

And then came professional hockey as we know it now, with the construction of mammoth rinks and the introduction of frankfurters in the lobbies. Every large city bought itself a hockey team to foster civic spirit, each team composed almost exclusively of Canadians, thereby making the thing a local matter—local to the North American continent, that is.

As at present played, hockey is a fast game, expert and clean, which gives the players plenty of chance to skate very fast from one end of a rink to the other and the spectators a chance to catch that cold in the head they have been looking for. Thousands of people flock to the arenas to witness the progress of the teams in the league and to cheer their fellow townsmen from Canada in their fierce rivalry with players, also from Canada, who wear the colors of Boston, New York, Detroit, and other presumptuous cities. As the number of cities which support hockey teams increases, the difficulty is going to come in impressing on the French-Canadian players the names of the cities they are playing for, so that they won't get mixed up in the middle of the game and start working for the wrong side. A Frenchman playing for Chillicothe or Amagansett will have to watch himself pretty carefully.

However, this is all beside the point—or beside the cover-point, if you want to be comical, even though there aren't any more cover-points. What this article set out to do was to explain how hockey may be watched with a minimum of discomfort and an inside knowledge of the finer points of the game.

As it is necessary to have ice in order to play ice-hockey, I have invented a system, now in use in most rinks, whereby an artificial ice may be made by the passage of ammonia through pipes and one thing and another. The result is much the same as regular ice except that you can't use it in high-balls. It hurts just as much to fall down on and is just as easily fallen on as the real thing. In fact, it *is* ice, except that—well, as a matter of fact, although I invented the thing I can't explain it, and, what is more, I don't *want* to explain it. If you don't already know what artificial ice is, I don't care if you never know.

If you arrive at the hockey game just a little bit late, you will be able to annoy people around you by asking what has taken place since the game began. There is a place where the score is indicated, it is true, but it is difficult to find, especially if you come in late. In the Madison Square Garden in New York, where every night some different kind of sport is indulged in (one night, hockey; the next night, prize-fighting; the next night, bicycle-racing; and so on and so forth) the same scoreboard is used except that the numbers are lighted up differently. I went to a hockey game late the other night and, looking up at the scoreboard, figured it out that Spandino and Milani had three more laps to go before they were three laps ahead of anyone else. This confused me a little, but not enough. I knew, in a way, that I was not at a bicycle race but I didn't feel in a position to argue with any scoreboard. So I went home rather than cause trouble.

Spectators at a hockey game, however, are generally pretty well up in the tactics of the game, always, as usual, excepting the women spectators. I would like to bet that a woman could have played hockey herself for five years and yet, if put among the spectators, wouldn't know what that man was

You can slip out and have a session with a frankfurter.

doing with the little round disc. However, poking fun at women for not knowing games is old stuff, and we must always remember that we men our- selves don't know everything about baking pop- overs. Not any more than women do. (Heh-heh!)

The man who thought of installing frankfurter stands in the lobbies of hockey arenas had a great idea. If it looks as if there might not be any scor- ing done for a long time (and, what with goal- tenders as efficient as they are, it most always does look that way) you can slip out and have a session with a frankfurter or even a bar of nougatine and get back in time to see the end of the period. The trouble with professional hockey as played today is that the goal-tenders are too good. A player may carry the puck down the ice as far as the goal and then, owing to the goal-tender's being just an old fool and not caring at all about the spectators, never get it in at all. This makes it difficult to get up any enthusiasm when you see things quickening up, because you know that nothing much will come of it anyway. My plan would be to eliminate the goal- tenders entirely and speed up the game. The offi- cials could help some by sending them to the penalty box now and then.

As a matter of fact, I have never even seen a hockey game in my whole life.

"I AM IN THE BOOK"

THERE are several natural phenomena which I shall have to have explained to me before I can consent to keep on going as a resident member of the human race. One is the metamorphosis which hats and suits undergo exactly one week after their purchase, whereby they are changed from smart, intensely becoming articles of apparel into something children use when they want to "dress up like daddy." Another is the almost identical change undergone by people whom you have known under one set of conditions when they are transferred to another locale.

Perhaps the first phenomenon, in my case, may be explained by the fact that I need a valet. Not a valet to come in two or three times a week and sneak my clothes away, but a valet to follow me about, everywhere I go, with a whiskbroom in one hand and an electric iron in the other, brushing off a bit of lint here, giving an occasional *coup de fer* there, and whispering in my ear every once in a while, for God's sake not to turn my hat brim down that way. Then perhaps my hats and suits would remain the hats and suits they were when I bought them.

56

I need a valet to follow me about, everywhere I go.

But the second mysterious transformation—that of people of one sort into people of another sort, simply by moving them from one place to another in different clothes—here is a problem for the scientists; that is, if they are at all interested.

Perhaps I do not make myself clear. (I have had quite a bit of trouble that way lately.)   I will give an example if you can get ten other people to give, too. Let us say that you went to Europe this summer. You were that rosy-faced man in a straw hat who went to Europe this summer. Or you went to the seashore. My God, man, you must have gone *somewhere!*

Wherever you were, you made new acquaintances, unless you had whooping cough all the time. On the voyage home, let us say, you sat next to some awfully nice people from Grand Rapids, or were ill at practically the same time as a very congenial man from Philadelphia. These chance acquaintances ripened into friendships, and perhaps into something even more beautiful (although I often think that *nothing* is really more beautiful than friendship), and before long you were talking over all kinds of things and perhaps exchanging bits of fruit from your steamer baskets. By the day before you landed you were practically brother and sister—or, what is worse, brother and brother.

"Now we must get together in the fall," you say. "I am in the book. The first time you come to town give me a ring and we'll go places and see things." And you promise to do the same thing whenever you happen to be in Grand Rapids or Philadelphia.

Before long you were exchanging bits of fruit from your baskets.

You even think that you might make a trip to Grand Rapids or Philadelphia especially to stage a get-together.

The first inkling you have that maybe you won't quite take a trip to Grand Rapids or Philadelphia is on the day when you land in New York. That morning everyone appears on deck dressed in traveling clothes which they haven't worn since they got on board. They may be very nice clothes and you may all look very smart, but something is different. A strange tenseness has sprung up and everyone walks around the deck trying to act natural, without any more success than seeming singularly unattractive. Some of your bosom friends, with whom you have practically been on the floor of the bar all the way over, you don't even recognize in their civilian clothes.

"Why, look who's here!" you say. "It's Eddie! I didn't know you, Eddie, with that great, big, beautiful collar on." And Eddie asks you where you got that hat, accompanying the question with a playful jab in the ribs which doesn't quite come off. A rift has already appeared in the lute and you haven't even been examined yet by the doctors for trachoma.

By the time you get on the dock and are standing around among the trunks and dogs, you may catch sight of those darling people, the Dibbles, standing in the next section under "C," and you wave weakly and call out, "Don't forget, I'm in the book!" but you know in your heart that you could be in a book of French drawings and the Dibbles wouldn't look you up—which is O. K. with you.

Sometimes, however, they do look you up. Perhaps you have parted at the beach on a bright morning in September before you went up to get dressed for the trip to the city. The Durkinses (dear old

Durkinses!) were lying around in their bathing suits and you were just out from your last swim preparatory to getting into the blue suit.

"Well, you old sons-of-guns," you say, smiling through your tears, "the minute you hit town give us a ring and we'll begin right where we left off. I know a good place. We can't swim there, but, boy, we can get wet!"

At which Mr. and Mrs. Durkins scream with laughter and report to Mr. and Mrs. Weffer, who are sitting next, that you have said that you know a place in town where you can't swim but, boy, you can get wet. This pleases the Weffers, too, and they are included in the invitation.

"We'll have a regular Throg's Point reunion," Mrs. Weffer says. Mrs. Weffer isn't so hot at making wisecracks, but she has a good heart. Sure, bring her along!

Along about October you come into the office and find that a Mr. Durkins has called and wants you to call him at his hotel. "Durkins? Durkins? Oh, *Durkins!* Sure thing! Get me Mr. Durkins, please." And a big party is arranged for that night.

At six o'clock you call for the Durkinses at their hotel. (The Weffers have lost interest long before this and dropped out. The Durkinses don't even know where they are—in Montclair, New Jersey, they think.) The Durkinses are dressed in their traveling clothes and you are in your business suit, such as it is (such as *business* is). You are not quite sure that it *is* Mrs. Durkins at first without that yellow sweater she used to wear all the time at the beach. And Mr. Durkins looks like a house-detective in that collar and tie. They both look ten years older and not very well. You have a feeling that you look pretty seedy, too.

"Well, well, here we are again! How are you all?"

"Fine and dandy. How are you—and the missus?"

"Couldn't be better. She's awfully sorry she couldn't get in town tonight. (You haven't even told her that the Durkinses were here.) What's the news at dear old Throg's Point?"

"Oh, nothing much. Very dead after you left."

"Well, well— (A pause.) How have you *been* anyway, you old son of a gun?"

"Oh, fine; fine and dandy! You all been well?"

"Couldn't be better. What was going on at the old dump when you left? Any news? Any scandal?"

"Not a thing."

"Well, well— Not a thing, eh?— Well, that's the way it goes, you know; that's the way it goes."

The general atmosphere is that of a meeting in a doctor's office.

"Yes, sir, I guess you're right— You look fine."

"Feel fine—I could use a little swim right now, though."

"Oh, boy, couldn't I though!" (The weather being very cold for October, this is recognized by both sides as an entirely false enthusiasm, as neither of you ever really cared for swimming even in summer.)

"How would you like to take a walk up to Sammy's for a lobster sandwich, eh?"

"Say, what I couldn't do to one right now! *Boy!* Or one of those hot dogs!"

"One of Sammy's hot dogs *wouldn't* go bad right now, you're right."

"Well, well— You've lost all your tan, haven't you?"

"Lost it when I took my first hot-water bath."

This gets a big laugh, the first, and last, of the evening. You are talking to a couple of strangers and the conversation has to be given adrenalin every three minutes to keep it alive. The general atmosphere is that of a meeting in a doctor's office.

It all ends up by your remembering that, after dinner, you have to go to a committee meeting which may be over at nine o'clock or may last until midnight and they had better not wait for you. You will meet them after the theatre if you can. And you know that you can't, and *they* know that you can't, and, what is more, they don't care.

So there you are! The example that I gave has been rather long; so there isn't much room left for a real discussion of the problem. But the fact remains that people are one thing in one place and another thing in another place, just as a hat that you buy in the store for a natty gray sport model turns out to be a Confederate general's fatigue-cap when you get it home. And if you know of any explanation, I don't care to hear about it. I'm sick of the subject by now anyway.

A SHORT HISTORY OF AMERICAN POLITICS

THOSE of you who get around to reading a lot will remember that a history of American politics was begun by me several chapters back —or rather, an introduction to such a history was written. Then came the Great War . . . brother was turned against brother, father against father; the cobblestones of the Tuileries were spattered with the blood of the royalists, and such minor matters as histories were cast aside for the musket and ploughshare. In crises such as that of March, 1928, the savants must give way to the men of action.

Now that the tumult and the shouting have died, however, the history of American politics can be written. The only trouble at present is that I have lost the introduction I wrote several months ago. It must have fallen down behind the bureau and the wall of the Kremlin.

To write another introductory preface would be silly, and that is the reason I have decided to write one. The other one was probably not much good, anyway. So while you all go ahead and read the

other pages of this volume, I will write another
introduction to a history of American politics.
(That is, I will if I can get this stuff off the keys
of my typewriter. Either somebody has rubbed
candy over each key while I have been dozing here
or the typewriter itself has a strain of maple in it
and is giving off sap. I have never run across anything like it in all my experience with typewriters.
The "j" key looks so sticky that I am actually afraid
to touch it. Ugh!)

Well, anyway——

A History of American Politics

(2 vol., 695 pp. 8vo...................100 to 1 to show.)

INTRODUCTION

The theory of political procedure in those countries in which a democratic form of government ob-
tains is based on the assumption that the average
citizen knows enough to vote. (*Time out for prolonged laughter.*)

The Ideal State of Plato, as you will remember
(you liar!), was founded on quite a different principle, but, if you will look at Greece today you will
see that something was wrong in that principle, too.
Plato felt—and quite rightly—that Truth is the

Ultimate Good and that the Ultimate Good is Truth —or the Idea. (Check one of these three.) *Now*— in the Ideal State, granted that the citizens keep away from the polls and mind their own business, we have an oligarchy or combination of hydrogen atoms so arranged as to form Truth in the Abstract. Of course, Plato wrote only what he had learned from Socrates, and Socrates, like the wise old owl that he was, never signed his name to anything. So that left Plato holding the bag for an unworkable political theory which has been carried down to the present day.

Aristotle followed Plato with some new theories, but as he dealt mostly with the Drama and Mathematics, with side excursions into Bird Raising and Exercises for the Eye, we don't have to bother with his ideas on Government. I don't remember what they were, in the first place.

This brings us up to 1785, when the United States began to have its first political prickly-heat. It may have been a little before 1785 (I am working entirely without notes or reference books in this history), but 1785 is near enough, for the Revolution didn't end until around 1782, or 1780, and that would leave a couple of years for George Washington to begin his two terms as President and get things good and balled up. So we will say 1785.

Here we are, then, a new country, faced with an experiment in government and working on nothing sounder than a belief that the average voter is entitled to have a hand in the running of the State. The wonder is that we have got as far as we have —or *have* we?

Now, in this introduction I have tried to outline the main influences in political thought which culminated in the foundation of our form of government. I have omitted any reference to Lebœuf and Froissart, because, so far as I know, Lebœuf and Froissart never had any ideas on the subject; at any rate, not the Lebœuf that I knew. I have not gone into the Hanseatic League or the Guild System, not through any pique on my part, but because, after all, they involved a quite different approach to the question of democratic government and I couldn't find any pictures which would illustrate them interestingly. If, however, any of my readers are anxious to look up the Hanseatic League, I can refer them to a very good book on the subject called "The Hanseatic League."

I can not bring to a close this preface to my history, inadequate as it is, without acknowledging the customary debt of gratitude to France.

THE BRIDGE OF SANS GENE

Being a Report of the European Hike of Gene
Tunney and Thornton Wilder, Written in
the Manner of One of Them—You
Must Guess Which

PART ONE

Don Gene

THE reputation of Don Gene Tunney, *campeón del mundo,* arose from three sources: a powerful right, a roving left, and an incurable reverence for the classics. Citizens who had seen him fighting in the prize-ring doubted that he could read; those who had seen him under a catalpa tree with a book doubted that he could fight. And yet Don Gene went on fighting and reading, pleasing nobody, least of all his opponents.

His mind was filled with naïve speculations: as to the authenticity of the second half of "A Winter's Tale"; as to the all-but-obscured date on the first folio of Machiavelli's "Prince"; as to the probable course and potential discomfort of the freckled fist belonging to the new *Desfiador*. To all of these, and many more problems, Don Gene turned an ingenuous attention. And, in the meantime he lived immaculately, read much, and punched a large, harassed leather bag.

It was not strange, therefore, that people who read but little themselves, or those who lived maculately, or those who punched no bags, should look askance at this young man who did all three. There is no more suspicious character in the world, nor one more worthy of ill-natured surveillance, than the man whose life is an open book.

PART TWO

El Novelista

Members of the American Academy at Rome at the beginning of the third decade of the Twentieth Century recall a quiet young man named Wilder who wrote. Everyone knew that one day he would do something great and everyone was very kind and misunderstanding. And so when, a little later, the young man finished an excellent novel, there was great searching of hearts among the members of the American Academy at Rome; for it was found that the novel was dedicated to them. As is often the case with excellent books, this one was read by such as were implicated, by the young man's relatives, and by nobody else.

El Novelista Wilder re-introduced delicacy in style to a world which had long been living in squalid sin with realism; he re-wrote his first drafts; he polished his adjectives with meticulous and loving care; he took pains with his work in violation of all the rules of his craft. Later he was to have the distinction of being the first writer in history who, having described one of his characters as being master of lovely phrases, proceeded to fortify his description by actually giving her lovely phrases to use. It is true, in his first book he affected a confusing disdain for quotation-marks; but the thoughts of youth are long, long thoughts and as youth grows older its thoughts come closer.

From Rome *Novelista* Wilder emerged with a modest knowledge of mankind, a curiosity as to its navigation, and a commission to instruct the youth of his native land in such matters as he himself had learned at the supple knee of William Lyon Phelps. Peace was in him; things were not going badly. Serene in his conviction that he had presuffered the penalties of gregariousness, he settled down to a platonic strolling through academic groves; he took his time; eventually he wrote another book, which, because of its exquisite treatment of certain Peruvian eccentrics, was awarded a prize for the novel best fostering the standards of North American home-life.

PART THREE

The Prize-Writer and the Prize-Fighter

How it was that Don Gene Tunney and *El Novelista* came to cross the sea together, nobody knew; how it was that they ever met at all, nobody seemed able to say. It was one of those spectacular partnerships by which Nature proves that she knows her Thoreau. Only those who have walked can ride; only those who have ridden can walk.

And so it was that one warm afternoon late in the third decade of the Twentieth Century the two were overheard in conversation as they sat resting under the hedge which bordered the estate of Don Speranza Machihembrada y Pegujalero. Don Speranza, being a man of affairs, happened to be in his garden opening letters; he listened to the voices for two reasons: first because they interested him; second, his alternative was to listen to the voice of his conscience, always a tiring conversationalist.

"It seems to me," one voice was saying, "that if Shakespeare had meant 'Nerissa' to imply suicide he would have written it into the play. I cannot take Royce's notation as an established fact."

The other voice waited; there was a pause.

"A short punch is sometimes more effective than a wide swing," the second voice was speaking now. "Look, if you will, at the blow which settled the South American Firpo. Not more than a six-inch arc."

"A literary man *en tour* with a boxer," said Don Speranza to himself. "An odd combination; or perhaps not so odd. I will see for myself and perhaps add them to my collection." Don Speranza had the second finest collection of ivory rabbits in all Spain; the other, and still finer collection, belonged to him also.

The first voice spoke again; it told of the theory held by Gilbert Murray that in Book 22, Line 52 of the Iliad the comma should come *after δομοισιν*, making it read "Sorrow"; of the contemporary account which told of Milton's being drunk, not blind; of the lost page of Tasso which held the key to the puzzling use of the subjunctive in dealing with Orlando's love for Wordsworth's "Lucy."

To these, and many other, observations the second voice interposed its owner's belief that within two more rounds in Chicago Dempsey would have gone to his long home; that a "one-two," if properly timed, is the most effective form of fisticuff;

that the "rabbit-punch," no matter how prolonged, serves only as an incentive to its victim.

On hearing these words as he made his way through the hedge, Don Speranza gave thought to the problem of salutation which confronted him. "The one who speaks of Shakespeare and Tasso," he said to himself, "must be the literary man. Being a literary man myself, having written a preface to the Granada edition of 'Pepita Jimenez,' I will address myself to him first." It will be seen from this that Don Speranza thought things out; his mind was two-edged and keen; he also had the third finest collection of ivory rabbits in all Spain.

Now according to all satirical badinage in the land of Don Gene's birth, where he was known as the reading-fighter or the fighting-reader, this account should end with Don Speranza's discovery that the one who spoke of Shakespeare and Tasso was the boxer; that the one who spoke of fisticuffs, the writer. Such tales have a way of so ending. But life itself has a confusing tendency to be conventional; life itself is possessed of little satire. And Don Speranza was right; it was *El Novelista* who spoke of Milton; the one who recalled Dempsey was Don Gene, the boxer. And so all three made merry until long after sundown; *El Novelista* telling of Chaucer; Don Gene of Heeney; Don Speranza of ivory rabbits, of which he had the fourth finest collection in all Spain.

Some say that we shall never know what to think about our fellowmen, and some say, on the contrary, that the world is a crystal for those who will look into it. And why should it not be so; or, if you will, why should it?

TRY-OUTS

BETWEEN the closing of one theatrical season and the opening of the next ("comes a pause in the day's occupations that is known as the Children's Hour") several hundred plays are "tried out" in the provinces to see what they need before being brought into New York. It is usually found that they need amputation just below *and* just above the knee. Not enough of them, however, are thrown into the incinerator after the try-out. The managements of many of them seem to have some ingenuous idea that they can be "fixed" and that they will then knock the metropolis cold. "The third act needs a little rewriting," they say hopefully, "and we need someone else as the parson, but aside from that we're set." And there is another drama lined up for us slaves of the public to write an obituary for.

Avid, as usual, for news, this department has been spending these hot summer weeks going about the Atlantic seaboard spying on abortive dramatic entertainments in the outlying districts, with an eye (sometimes one eye, sometimes two) for possible metropolitan material in the fall. And we must admit that, so far as we have seen, nothing is fit to come into New York at all.

Take, for example, the show put on for the benefit of the Yacht Club at Si... ..t, Rhode Island. It was called "The Sinosset Follies of 1928," a title implying that there have been others like it in years past and are likely to be more in the future. Reason totters at the very thought of such a sequence. We have laws against liquor and smallpox. Are the "Sinosset Follies" going to be allowed to run their course year after year? It were better that the Sinosset Yacht Club fell into decay like the castles of the Rhineland than that such a thing should be perpetuated.

The opening chorus of "The Sinosset Follies" consisted of six young men and six young ladies in yachting costume (or what passes in Sinosset as a yachting costume). The lyric to this chorus was written by J. Foster Wrenn, Chairman of the Entertainment Committee and a perfect peach of a chap who, had Fate not made him an indifferent architect, would most certainly have given both the Gershwin brothers a run for their money. All the lyrics in the show, you will find, were written by J. Foster Wrenn, and based on existing lyrics by Lorenz Hart and Buddy De Sylva. Mr. Wrenn also coached the show and worked awfully, awfully hard to make it a success, and everybody ought to be awfully grateful to him—or else take a good sock at him.

The opening chorus is followed (after a short wait while the back-drop is disentangled from the borders) by a sketch showing one of the less attractive phases of social life in Sinosset, intelligible only to very old Sinossetites and not very pleasing even to them. The author of the sketch is not mentioned, and the supposition is that the actors are making it up as they go along. Then comes a number in which a young lady and young gentleman sing and, what is even worse, dance to, "You Took Advantage of Me," for which they can be prosecuted and sent to jail by the management of "Present Arms!" now running in New York. And if the management of "Present Arms!" have any social conscience at all they will hire Clarence Darrow and spend millions on the prosecution. This department will head a subscription list with $100 right now.

When "The Sinosset Follies of 1928" breaks up at a quarter before one in the morning, its patrons have been treated to three paraphrases of current popular songs, two very long monologues (one of which was fortunately cut short in the middle by the monologist's falling off the platform and disappearing for good), a finale to the first part, a finaletto, a grand finale to the whole show involving fourteen more people than the stage would hold, and four comedy sketches based on topical Sinosset situations which were not essentially dramatic in themselves and which, even had they been excerpts from "The Wild Duck," would have lacked a certain something as entertainment. These were interspersed with rather long announcements by J. Foster Wrenn in person, who, in common with three or four thousand amateur announcers throughout the country, had seen M. Balieff on his first appearance in this country and had been known as the local "Balieff" ever since for no discernible reason. This epidemic of amateur Balieffs is one of the major harms done this country by the introduction of the Chauve-Souris eight years ago.

As it was rumored back-stage that a representative of Ziegfeld and one of the Shuberts in person were out front looking for possible metropolitan material all of the actors were in great form and doing their best, which, unfortunately, was not quite good enough.

We have singled out "The Sinosset Follies of 1928" because it is representative of a type of entertainment which is going on all summer from Maine to—what is the name of that state?—Cali-

He had been known as the local "Balieff" ever since.

fornia, but other productions which we have seen in our tour of inspection have just as little chance of getting into New York in the fall. Among them we may list the revival of "Pinafore" given, much to the disgust of Messrs. Gilbert and Sullivan, by the summer colony at Eagle Lake, Michigan; a kermess entitled, "Around the World with the Roses," which had the ostensible excuse of providing recreation for the indigent pets of Santa Ira, California; and, as bad as any of them, a performance of "Within the Law" given by a summer stock company composed of "guest stars" from Broadway who were taking their vacations by not learning their lines for a new show each week.

The fact that the Drama survives the body-blows given it by amateur and professional organizations each summer should be proof enough that it is an essential feature of our civilization. It *should* be proof enough, but, for us, it isn't.

AFRICAN SCULPTURE

Its Background, Future and the Old-Fashioned Waltz

(With Photographs by the Author)

THE recent exhibition of West African sculpture created a furor in art circles which died down in about fifteen minutes—which was just about the time consumed in removing the *objets* from the packing crates. We are therefore printing a critical estimate of these little carvings in an attempt to arouse enough interest in them among art lovers to have them crated up again to be sent back to West Africa.

One must understand the spirit which is at the back of West African sculpture in order to appreciate the intense *integrity* of its technique. It isn't so much the sculpture itself (although, in a way, it *is*) as the fact that it is filled with raisins. These can be extracted and eaten if you like raisins. Early Florentine sculpture and late Greek modeling (some of the late Greek was so late that it ran right over into Early Florentine and nobody knew the difference) had no raisins.

A study of the examples printed on this page will hardly serve to demonstrate this point, but it won't do any harm to look at them casually.

Example 1 is a native West African funeral mask, worn by any relative of the deceased who wanted to attend the funeral and yet didn't want the rest of the relatives to know that he was in town. This would probably account for the strong Irish cast to the features of the mask. No one would think of an Irishman being a relative of a native West African, although stranger things *have* happened. This mask was brought back by the Huber's 42nd St. Museum expedition and is now on exhibition in the Renaissance Biped Room of the Museum itself.

Example 2 is one of the most sincere of these native sculptures. It is a local fetish in the shape of a salt-cellar (a pretty funny shape for a salt-cellar, you are doubtless saying to yourself), as salt is considered to be very lucky on the West Coast of Africa, especially if you happen to have any fried chicken and hashed-in-cream potatoes to put it on. This salt-cellar fetish, in addition to being a talisman, also tells a story (stop it if you have heard it):

It represents the gradual growth of the seed to the mature plant, the seed being represented by the two hands of the little figure and the mature plant

Funeral mask, worn by relatives who want to look Irish.

by the two knees. In the spring of the year, when the seed is planted, everything is bright and green. Hence the hands. In the fall, when the grain is garnered, the year is nearing its close, Nature is putting on her winding sheet for the long winter, and nothing seems right. Hence the knees. That may not be the explanation at all. How should *I* know?

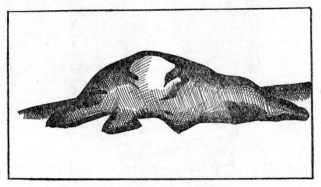

This doesn't seem to mean much to any one.

Example 3 is a poser, frankly. It was found on the West Coast, in a district known as the "West Coast Studios." Nobody seems to know who found this example of native art, or where it was found. It just turned up among some other bits of sculpture in the Museum's shipment. At first it was thought to be a bust of the local Lon Cha . . . Beg pardon! At first it was thought to be a replica

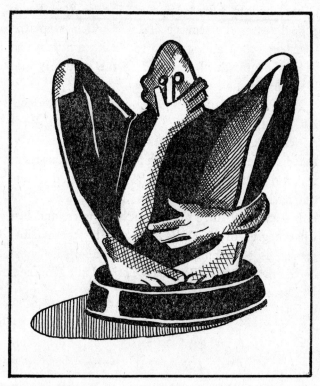

West African salt-cellar fetish, showing the growth of grain
from the seedling to the ripe kernel.

of Naa, the Fog-God—and it still may be. The argument against this theory is that it isn't round enough. Other experts have placed it in the Post-Fever School (after the scourge of fever which swept the Coast in 1780) and seem to see in it an attempt to show the growth of the seed to the mature grain. Here, again, finders are keepers.

Now, a study of these three examples, representing, as they do, three distinct schools of West African sculptural art, shows us one thing—namely, that long before the coming of the White Man there was a distinct feeling for æsthetic expression among the natives of that section of the continent. Just how successful these savage strivings were, and just what degree of skill was mastered by these tribal artists, is something which each connoisseur must decide for himself. Personally, I wouldn't give them houseroom.

FOOTBALL SAGAS

THERE has got to be a drastic deflation in style among football-reporters, otherwise the sports-writers are going to find themselves swirling through space on comets, with bulging eyes and throbbing temples, trying to find newer and more ecstatic ways of saying, "Yale and Harvard played football yesterday."

The language of football reporting has become so exalted in the past few years that the only thing left will be to have the noble words which the sports-writers have written set to music and chanted by a male choir in white vestments from the top of Bald Mountain at dusk. Compared with the phrases used to describe the most tepid of mid-season games the Latin cadences dealing with rosy-fingered Aurora and her ilk sound like stock-market quotations. When "twenty-two young Titans face each other in a battle the echoes of which will ring down through the centuries as long as man tells tales of valor and cunning," it is time to give pause and see if, by chance, we are not living in the Golden Age of Heroes and don't know it.

When even so unemotional a paper as the New

York *Times* soars to stylistic heights as it did in Mr. Danzig's account of one Yale-Princeton game and we learn that "never had any in that tremendous gathering ever come to a game with fonder expectations of seeing a struggle to go down the ages . . . and never were expectations more fully realized than they were in this battle between two stalwart lines and two brilliant back-fields—a battle which reached so feverish a heat and which had so startling a dénouement that the most generous impulses were smothered down in the vivid flame of partisanship kindled by the desperateness of the conflict and the turns of fortune. It was a game to live forever in the memories of a gathering which went through a gamut of emotions perhaps never exceeded in the experience of a football crowd"—when the *Times* does that, what are we to expect of such susceptible word-poets as Grantland Rice? The "perhaps" in the last sentence is the only sign of the *Times'* traditional conservatism. Having said "*perhaps* never exceeded" they can not be sued for libel at any rate.

We have seen "an autumn sky heavily tinted with flames and flashes of orange and black turn suddenly into the shining glow of Yale's triumphant blue" (Grantland Rice saw this phenomenon and told the *Herald Tribune* readers of it) and in four out of eight accounts of this same titantic struggle we found that "twenty-two giants battled" for supremacy in what looks like the most stupendous conflict since Olympus was closed.

When the heroic mood is not on the writers they adopt the narrative style of Ralph Henry Barbour in his "For the Honor of the School" series. Mr. James Robbins, in the *World,* began his story of an Army-Notre Dame game as follows:

"Out in the black and gold of the Army trod a lone ball-catcher. Veterans had failed in what he was to do. The score was Army 6; Notre Dame o. . . .

" 'Seven—eleven—twenty-two!' began the Notre Dame quarter. It was John (Butch) Niemiec's number being called—Niemiec, the deadly passer.

"Back of the other line was a youth who had sat an idle sideline slave, but a tiny orb among the scintillating stars, the knights of West Point castle. He was William Lester Nave, from Cleveland. He had been put in to catch the ball.

" 'It can't be done, but we'll try,' thought his team-mates.

"Bill crouched for a spring. His heels were off the grass.

" 'He will!' shrieked a girl's voice from the grand-stand.

"Back snapped the ball. Twenty-one players in combat. Heels-over-head they tumbled as they met and lifted up.

"Off from the flying tangle was the lone ball-catcher. Over came the spiraling ball.

"Another cry rent the air above the grandstand.

" 'Bill!' it seemed to implore.

"Into the waiting arms of Nave, the young knight, came the oval. His arms steeled it and he jumped ahead. . . . Off he pushed three opponents, straight-arming them away. Forty-five yards he covered before they brought him down at the goal-line.

"A crunching of flesh was untangled. A shout! A roar! A touchdown! Nave was over the line. A substitute!

"Cheer on cheer like volleyed thunder burst forth from the Army side. It was Nave! Nave! NAVE!

"So the tide of strife was turned at the Yankee Stadium where West Point humbled the lads of Notre Dame 18-0."

Of course, the fact that the Army was already one touchdown ahead when the substitute made this run detracts a little from Mr. Robbins' plot, but having the girl in the grandstand was nothing short of inspiration on his part.

Another favorite bit of word-wizardry among the

sporting writers (initiated, I believe, by Mr. McGee-han a long time ago) is taking the hero of a game and referring to him throughout the story by his full names, Christian, middle and given. This was an effective gag at first, but when, week after week, we find some one player singled out in each game for this distinction, players whose names are never heard again, even during the same season, it loses a little of its vigor as a writing ruse. Perhaps an example is not necessary, and yet we have a perfect one at hand in the *Times* account of the Army-Notre Dame game already mentioned (oddly enough Mr. Harrison picks out an entirely different hero from the one immortalized by Mr. Robbins in the *World,* which only goes to show that even two sporting writers at the same game are unaware of exactly which one of the twenty-two Titans is to go ringing down through the ages). Here is Mr. Harrison's version:

"A red-headed half-back, who plods along only a trifle faster than that ancient sprinter Mercury, wrote finis across the championship aspirations of Notre Dame yesterday. . . . The fleet-footed lad in question is carried on the official records as Christian K. Cagle, but up at the Point he is better known as plain ordinary Red. He was the hero of a game that abounded in heroes. . . . Near the end of the game Christian K. Cagle grabbed a beautiful forward pass. . . . And so what with one thing and another, including Christian K. Cagle, and a score of other sturdy youths from up West Point way, Notre Dame was outplayed," etc.

Perhaps it would be well for them all to go back to the simple direct style with which George Daley in the *World* led into his story of a Yale-Princeton game:

"One bold, unexpected play by Johnny Hoben which tangled up and crossed the Tigers was directly responsible for Yale's football victory over Princeton here today by a score of 14 to 6."

At any rate, Mr. Daley tells us right at the start who won.

MR. MENCKEN REVIEWS MR. NATHAN
AND VICE VERSA

(with apologies, in German, to both)

The Literary Katzenjammer

ART OF THE NIGHT, by George Jean Nathan. $2.50;
$10. 13½ x 6⅞. New York: *Alfred A. Knopf.*

A MONG the more illuminating manifestations
of that imbecilic ratiocination peculiar to the
mens Americana is the belief, prevalent in some
quarters of our fair land, that Mr. George Jean
Nathan is a writer of importance. For preposterous rubbish this is comparable only with the more
august imbecility which rates Calvin Coolidge as a
great man, Offenbach as a great composer, or salted
almonds as great *Vorspeise.*

That Nathan is energetic can not be denied. That
he is privy to the sonorous hocus-pocus of critical
jargon is a fact patent to anyone who has had the
time and stomach to delve into the *Jahrbuch* issued
each spring under his name by the obliging House of
Knopf. Each contains current forms of prayer to
O'Neill, Ziegfeld, O'Casey and other gods, together

with expurgatoriana for the year's dæmons. But that these collections of *obiter dicta* furnish any more lasting contribution to the world's thought than is offered in the highfalutin rumble-bumble of Otto H. Kahn or the pish-posh incidental to the performance of the marriage service in the Church of England is an admission I am not prepared to make.

There is a current and quite preposterous impression that Nathan's hold on the intellectual booberie is a sensual one. He is supposed to titillate their nerve-centers, causing them to jump. More palpable tosh than this has not formed a part of the public superstition since the Sermon on the Mount. As a matter of fact, Nathan's appeal is spiritual. Assuming the manner of a cynical fellow, he looks sourly and with a bilious eye on the idols in the temple, but, even as he looks, he beats time to the chant of the priests and eventually, overcome with the religious razzle-dazzle, breaks into a profuse sweat, raises his arms to the heavens and performs a slow, reverent hoochie-koochie, followed by hundreds of zany converts.

To say that Nathan is a purveyor of sensory stimuli because he writes of beer-guzzling and hip-shaking is as much rubbish as to say that Aimée Semple McPherson is a purveyor of spiritual balm because she haggles with God, that a Shubert chorus man is a disciple of Karl Marx because he affects a red necktie or that Calvin Coolidge is a statesman because he wears a frock coat. If Nathan is an iconoclast, then Henry Ford makes automobiles and Otto H. Kahn has a dress-suit.

Since we find, then, that, in so far as Nathan is a force at all he is a spiritual force, he must stand back-to-back with his brother ballyhoo boys in the vineyards of the Lord and be measured. And, in competition with Rabbi Stephen S. Wise and Bishop Manning, Mr. Nathan can not hope ever to rise above the rank of drum-major's assistant. I confidently predict that in a hundred years he will be remembered solely for his cravats.

CLINICAL NOTES

By GEORGE JEAN NATHAN

*T*HE NEW MOSES.—Every now and again the
critical boys, many of them still in their emo-
tional didies themselves, get to cutting up over
some new baby they have found sucking at a bulrush
down by the river's bank. Here, they cry, is someone who is going to make Voltaire look like an
empty seidel of Löwenbräu, Daumier like a small
Emmenthaler *käse*, Brahms like an old Fedora hat
and John Singer Sargent like the wet end of a Bock
panetela. Such a phenomenon seems to be Professor
Henry L. Mencken, who, my trusted Egyptian body-
servant and spy tells me, is now being hailed as the
New Hot Dickety.

Aside from the local critics, who allow themselves
to be hornswoggled with a regularity and amiability
which could bring them in money if properly applied,
Le Mencken seems to have a following made up of
such giant intellects as believe that Cabell is better
than Rachmaninoff, Sinclair Lewis better than
Stravinsky, Dreiser better than Mestrović, O'Neill
better than Tunney, Dreiser better than O'Neill,

Lewis better than Dreiser, Cabell better than Lewis,
O'Neill better than Dreiser, and Sinclair Lewis better
than James Branch Cabell.

I have also reason to believe that under cross-
examination they would confess to a sneaking suspicion that (1) all hack-drivers are Swedenborgians;
(2) when a man asks a woman to marry him, she
always thinks he is fooling and accepts him; (3)
that if you cut the pages of a book with your finger
it makes the book look as if the pages had been cut
with someone's finger, and (4) that all hack-drivers
are Swedenborgians.

From such intellectual brothels, then, are the
Mencken witnesses assembled.   The State rests.

Etude in E Minor.—It is occasionally my duty,
as Liaison Officer for the Watch and Ward Society,
to look into the state of the *res publicæ* with special
reference to *sauce rémoulade*. I have been especially interested, therefore, in the pronunciamento
of several of my critical colleagues in New York that
the best *sauce rémoulade* is to be found at the Colony
Restaurant. This I take to be piffle and recommend
to my brothers in the bond that they look into the
sauce rémoulade in the oyster-bar at Prunier's in
Paris, at the Restaurant Horscher in Berlin, at
Schöner's in Vienna, at Hetlig's Café in Budapest,

at the Hotel zum Eisenhut in Rothenburg, at Louie's in Prague, and at the Central House in Bellows Falls, Vt.

Reprise.—It is my private opinion that Florenz Ziegfeld should receive the portfolio of Secretary of State without further shilly-shallying. As a picker of cuties, Kellogg has shown himself a dud.

THE NEW SOCIAL BLIGHT

ONE of the big questions which is agitating society today is why I don't go out more to parties. You hear it on all sides. "What has become of Benchley?" they say; "we never see him around at people's houses any more."

There is one camp which claims that I am embarrassed in the presence of strangers because of some malformation, another that I shun my friends because of conspicuous pores, and still another that since I flunked my Alexander Hamilton finals I have taken to seclusion and will see no one. I have instructed my attorneys to deny all of these insinuations categorically.

The real reason is that society today has turned intellectual on me. You can't go out any more to parties without being asked questions on matters of general information. Immediately the supper dishes are cleared away someone comes out with a list of questions concerning famous characters in history or literature, and there's your evening— just sunk.

When I was younger, a party was a party, not a college-board examination. We used to sit around

You can't go out any more without being asked questions on
general information.

and kiss each other, or drop handkerchiefs, or get to fighting, and everything was just dandy. Sometimes even the rugs would be pushed back and the more nimble ones would wrestle about on the floor to music. Among the older boys and girls a deck of cards would be broken out, and everyone would enjoy an evening of re-nigging (not spelled right and I know it) and snarling at each other. This sometimes ran into money, which was not a bad idea provided it ran in the right direction. And whatever we did, almost anybody could do it. All that was necessary was a fairly good constitution and enough sobriety to keep from falling on your forehead.

But now everything is different. Someone, a few years ago, began a revival of an old high school game called Twenty Questions. This was considered pretty effete when I was a boy and was indulged in by only those who didn't have the virility to play Post Office and other sex games. There would be one room (the warmest) devoted to Twenty Questions, and the rest, those who had any pride in their heritage, went into the next room and flung themselves about in various health-giving activities.

But suddenly Twenty Questions became *de rigueur*. You must be able to guess what someone was thinking of (as if anyone cared), or you must think of names of cities which began with "W" (even less tantalizing), or you must take a paper and pencil and jot down answers to such questions as "What famous Phœnician general, well known for his alto singing, was responsible for the Second Punic War?"

From this last game has developed the present pernicious custom of just plain General Information. After a good warm, heavy dessert and a hot mug of coffee you are supposed to settle down in the library and tell who wrote the poem beginning "If Niobe were here tonight, the moon in all her glory would—etc." Young people, with red blood coursing through their systems, must sit around in a circle and tell each other who invented amalgam fillings and what president of the United States studied palmistry until he was eleven years old. The future of the race is being placed in the hands of young men and women who spend their evenings together trying to remember who wrote the music to *Il Rogobo* and how many dreens there are in a gross gambut. If you were to ask me what we are coming to, as a nation, I should reply: "I don't know, *I'm* sure."

And now, to make things worse, they have gotten out a book full of questionnaires; so that hostesses

This standing has been achieved through years of scowling and
walking very slowly with my hands behind my back.

who can't think up things to ask their guests can just turn to this book and have enough material to tire out several parties. There are questionnaires on literature, mining, engineering, bird calls, and comparative plumbing, and then ones on general information which include everything. In one of these General Information questionnaires, Question No. 1 may be "What have the following in common: Alcibiades, Pepin the Great, Walter von der Vogelweide, and William A. Douglas?" and Question No. 2 may be "What is the coefficient of linear expansion in a steam pipe at 1367 South Water street?"

Now, in college, I took what was known as the "classical course," which meant that I had no courses after Friday and none before eleven in the morning. In the "classical course" it was also understood that there was to be no monkeying with mathematics or any of those fly-by-night sciences. A gentleman's education was what I was to have—and what I got. And whenever, in after life, I want to know anything, I go right to the encyclopedia and look it up. There was nothing said in the specifications about being able to answer on the dot any questions that a hostess might see fit to ask me after dinner.

When a man has reached my age, he can't afford

to go around to parties being humiliated. I have, through certain studied facial expressions and a characteristic carriage, established a reputation for dignity and civic stability for myself. People have come to think of me as a pillar of some sort or other, a definite bulwark in the literary and social life of the community. This standing has been achieved through years of scowling and keeping quiet while others were talking, and by walking very slowly with my hands behind my back. I tried for a while wearing glasses to add to the effect, but I couldn't see with them on and kept tripping over things, which, in a way, detracted.

And now I am asked nightly to jeopardize this hard-earned reputation by sitting around and making a sap of myself in front of a lot of people. There isn't one of those questions that I couldn't find the answer to in five minutes if I really wanted to know it. But I have other things to take up my mind, and, until the present craze for general information dies down, I shall devote myself to my studies in the privacy of my own room. At present I am working on a rather slick bit of trickery by means of which I can run out in Canfield.

PASSPORT DOPE

IF you are planning to go abroad, it is easy to see that you must have a passport. They won't let you abroad without a passport or something to show to the man. If you haven't got a passport to show him, you can show him some of the snapshots you took at the beach last summer, but he would rather look at a passport. Who wouldn't?

The first step in getting a passport is to write to the State Department in Washington and ask them nicely for one. Following is a suggested form letter to the State Department:

May 29, 19—
(*Name of year.*)

DEAR STUBBY:

What a swell guy *you* turned out to be, letting me take that trolley Thursday night instead of telling me that the bus went right by the door! It took me an hour and a quarter to get to Butch's and when I got there nobody was home. So I went into Lester's and had a combination sandwich and let it go at that. The next time you want some fun, try getting my suitcase out of the rumble seat of the Chrysler.

Well, what's mine is yours. You know that.

Sincerely,
(*Name of applicant.*)

After sending this letter to the State Department, it will be necessary for you to wait until they answer you. This ought not to take more than a week, if you know what I mean. It will then be time enough for you to take the physical examination. This ought not to be much trouble, provided you have taken any kind of care of yourself, or of anybody else. It consists chiefly of informal folk dancing in and out of the examination-room while the State Department officials make sketches of you. The best of these sketches (which are none too good) are finished up on a stiff cardboard (3 x 4 is a very poor size and should be avoided) and sent to you at your home, together with paper for wrapping and mailing.

Now comes the hard part. This is called "getting a visa." Take the sketch which the passport officials have made of you and show it to the representatives of the foreign countries which you wish to visit. You will find them in their offices on every Whitsunday at 4 P.M. At 4:05 P.M. they go out to lunch until next Whitsunday, so you will have to work fast. They will probably not like the sketch and will make no bones of saying so. Or, better yet, they will not be in their offices and you can give the whole thing up as a bad job.

Anything else you want to do?

"ISLAND IRISH"

Being a Comedy "Treatment" of Defoe's "Robinson Crusoe" in the Best Manner of the Movie Gag-Men and Title Writers.

1. Subtitle: YOUNG "ROB" CRUSOE WHO WAS SO WARM-HEARTED HE HAD HEARTBURN.

SCENE 1. *Main Street of Dover, England, background of trees and old-fashioned edibles.* (*Fade in.*)

Rob Crusoe, swinging down the street, so intent on reading a book that he walks into a tree, to which he apologizes and continues reading and walking. Copy of "Three Men in a Boat." (*Close up.*)

2. Subtitle: MARY MALONE, THE VILLAGE BELLE, WHO WAS SO IRISH THE OTHER GIRLS TURNED GREEN WITH ENVY.

Mary, walking in the other direction, sees Rob and looks at him with evident scorn. She, too, walks into the tree and apologizes. This brings Rob and Mary together, apologizing to each other.

3. Spoken Title: "I'M SORRY; I THOUGHT YOU WERE A TREE, YOU WERE SO GREEN!"

Mary smiles and looks the other way. Rob smiles and looks the other way, too. Therefore, neither of them sees the other and they both pass by, Rob walking into a pond and Mary walking into a store where she buys three yards of gingham, thinking it is Rob. (*Fade out.*)

SCENE 2. *Living-room, Mary's home. Background of faucets and old things.* (*Fade in.*)

4. Subtitle: MARY'S HOME LIFE WAS JUST ABOUT AS PEACEFUL AS A LEFT-HANDED DRIVER'S CHARIOT-RACE DOWN A RIGHT-HANDED DRIVEWAY. (*Fade in.*)

Mary is setting the table for supper. She has on a topcoat with the buttons set the wrong way, suggesting poverty. She lets the butter-pads slide into the water glasses, suggesting just plain carelessness.

5. Subtitle: ROGER MALONE, AN IRISH SAILOR, WHO WAS SO CROOKED HE HAD CROSSED THE EQUATOR EIGHT TIMES.

Roger Malone, Mary's father, is washing his hands at the sink, and, on hearing the butter-pads drop into the water glasses, turns in a rage and throws the sink at Mary. She dodges, and good-naturedly shakes her finger at her father until it drops off.

Roger Malone smiles at his daughter and dries his hands on his derby hat. He walks over to the table and sits down, tucking his napkin in his collar. It is too tight a fit, so he takes his collar off. Still it is too tight, so he takes his skirt off. Then he has no place in which to tuck his napkin, so he puts his head through a hole in the table-cloth, upsetting all the dishes.

SCENE 3. *Background interior of Rob's home.*

6. Subtitle: THURLOW CRUSOE, ROB'S FATHER, WHO NEEDED ONLY SOME EGGS TO HAVE HAM AND EGGS, IF HE HAD SOME HAM.

Thurlow Crusoe buttering sandwiches for yesterday's picnic. As he spreads the butter some feathers from the bed get stuck on his thumb, and as he pulls the feathers off his thumb, he scrapes the butter off the bread with his elbow. This goes on for fifty feet.

Rob enters and stands looking at his father with a tender expression. He then takes down a shotgun from the wall and aims it at the old man. As he does so his eye lights on the calendar hanging on the wall.

Calendar showing month with date for opening of hunting season marked in pencil. Rob's finger shows present date which is three days before opening of season. (Close up.)

Rob puts gun back on wall sadly and goes over and pats his father on head, leaving an ugly welt. (*Fade out.*)

SCENE 4. *Fishing wharf at Dover. Background of masts and unpleasant fish odors.*

Basket containing five puppies. (*Close up.*)

7. Spoken title: "Dog-fish!"

Rob and Mary laugh and clamber down on the deck to play with the puppies. An evil face appears over a hatchway. (*Fade in.*)

8. Subtitle: "Snail-bite" Pete, First Mate, Who Was So Tough He Kept His Collar on with a Nail in His Neck.

Pete sneaks up behind the pair of young lovers, who have by now handled the puppies so much that three of them are sick, and very quietly slips the hawser off the dock and casts off. By the time the young couple look up, they are on a desert island.

Scene 5. *Sandy beach on a desert island.* (*Long shot.*)

9. Subtitle: Rob and Mary Had About as Much Chance of Getting Off This Island as a Prohibitionist Has of Getting Off a Good Joke.

Rob and Mary walking hand in hand along the beach. Rob stops to pick up a bit of seaweed and Mary, who is looking the other way, reaches for his hand again. Instead she takes hold of a crab which has been walking along the beach in the other direction, and thinking that one of *its* claws is Rob's hand, walks along oblivious of the substitution, talking and chatting. She finally looks down and sees what she has been walking with and indicates horror.

Rob in the meantime has discovered something in the sand and calls Mary back to see it.

Large footprint in sand. (*Close up.*)

Rob and Mary examine the footprint closely and Mary starts to dig at it.

10. Spoken title: "LOOK OUT! DON'T TOUCH IT! PERHAPS IT'S WHERE SOMEONE STEPPED ON LON CHANEY!"

Mary jumps back in horror while Rob shades his eyes and scans the horizon. In the distance a speck is seen. He grabs Mary by the hand and they start running after the speck.

SCENE 6. *Chase sequence.*

Rob and Mary tear along the beach, swinging sometimes to the left into the long grass, sometimes to the right into the ocean. Once they nearly upset and once they come within an inch of colliding with a large fish which is coming up the beach in the opposite direction.

As Rob and Mary approach the speck in the distance, the speck approaches them at the same rate, until its turns out to be two Revenue Agents who are running toward Rob and Mary to arrest them for being bootleggers. The four runners collide.

11. Spoken title: "IT WON'T BE LONG NOW!"

The agents seize Rob and Mary and signal for the revenue-cutter which appears around the point.

Scene 7. On Board Revenue Cutter "Delight." (*Semi-close up.*) Background of Knots and Whistles.

The Revenue Officer leads Rob and Mary across the deck and sends for the commander. While they are waiting, Rob empties his pocket-flask behind him into a pail of water. The ship's goat comes up, drinks the water and becomes intoxicated, rushing madly toward the hatchway just as the commander is coming up, causing a nasty spill.

Rob and Mary wait with terror-stricken countenances. Commander turns and faces them and is discovered to be Thurlow Crusoe, Rob's father, who has been an under-cover man for the Government all the time. He seems delighted to see the young people and gives them his blessing. Rob and Mary embrace and one of the sailors runs a flag up at the masthead. *Union Jack upside down, signifying "We need assistance!"* (*Fade out.*)

ON THE AIR

WHAT with General Motors, Palmolive Soap, and all the other commercial products going into the radio-broadcasting business and giving out high-class musical and literary numbers, it may soon be so that Mr. Toscanini will have to don a yellow slicker and carry a fish for Cod Liver Oil if he wants to get a hearing. This commercialization is killing us artists.

It almost killed Grandpa, the author of this essay, the other night, when, for General Motors, he prostituted his art and stepped in front of a microphone to talk precious words and literary nuggets out into the air for millions of unappreciative citizens to hear—and to shut off on. Grandpa isn't used to having such a big audience and it made him a little jittery.

The worst part about a radio audience is that it is so cold. You stand up in front of that pole and pull some of your best stuff right into it—and what do you get? Not even Magnolia. You get a stony silence that hasn't been equaled since they asked for a rising vote of thanks to Tad Jones at a Harvard Club dinner.

The leader is looking out the window and dreaming of the days when he thought he was going to be a drum-major.

The old boy who tried to neck one of the lions in front of the New York Public Library was up against a hot-blooded proposition compared to Grandpa Benchley when he tried to make a radio audience laugh. It is one of the most discouraging experiences I have ever had, not forgetting the time when I winked at the Queen Mother in London once. I am practically crushed and bleeding, and I may go in for writing the Incoming Ships Department in *The Wall Street Journal* as a result.

In the first place, you have to *rehearse* these broadcasting acts. You have to go around at about five o'clock in the afternoon of the day when you are "going on the air" and run over your number just as if somebody were going to hear it. The "studio" is full of people even at that time of the day, musicians, timekeepers, trainers, and managers (there are sixteen managers to every program, each one under the impression that he is boss), and you have to say your piece out loud and try not to look silly. It was all I could do to say my piece out loud. I gave up trying not to look silly right at the start.

Come with me into the broadcasting studio in the afternoon, just as the shadows are beginning to deepen, and let us wander, hand in hand, through Radio Land. A big room, with perhaps seventy-

five people in it roaming aimlessly about, just like
a *real* business office. What you are supposed to
do is to run over your number to see how long it
takes. Everyone has a stop-watch, including the
girl who checks your coat. And while the orchestra
is trying to find "*a*," and the boy who works the
dynamo is trying to find his helper, and the assistant
manager is trying to find the second assistant manager, and the sunshine is trying to find the roses,
you mutter in a low tone whatever it is you think
you are going to say that night while a lady holds
a stop-watch on you without even listening. She's
no fool. Her job is just to find out how long it takes.
She isn't paid for *listening* to a lot of junk. She
isn't even paid for *looking* at you.

All right. You say your piece and your rehearsal
is over. You find that you did it in 9-2/5 minutes
flat, on a wet track, too. That's great, they tell
you. The week before, Irvin Cobb did only 10 flat.
You then rush into the showers and have a rub-
down, followed by a test to see if your voice can be
heard in the next room. If they can't hear your
voice in the next room, there isn't much chance of
its being heard in Flagstaff, Arizona.

So you go into a little box and say the first paragraph over again, this time into what they jokingly
call the "mike." Sometimes you say it into the

"mike" and sometimes into the "pat," but it's always the same old story about the two Irishmen. Well, it turns out that your voice isn't much good. You must raise it a little—not louder, mind you, just higher. Or else you must lower it. Not softer, but deeper. Mr. Werrenrath, the celebrated Danny Deever hummer, was one of those in charge at my tryout and he made the big mistake of telling me that I ought to make my voice sound more like a nance. " 'Way up here," he said, indicating where he puts "The Road to Mandalay" when he isn't using it, " 'way up here in the roof of the mouth." So I socked him and left in a huff. Mr. Werrenrath ought to know better than that.

I was told to come back at nine, as the concert was to begin at nine-thirty. Just what I was supposed to do between nine and nine-thirty I never could figure out, because if there ever was a dull period in the world's activities it is while people are waiting to begin a radio program. You can't even peek out through the curtain and see who is coming in—because there is nobody coming in.

We all got in a little room, the orchestra, the male quartet, six representatives of the advertising agency who were running the show, a delegation of rooters from General Motors, and a dozen substitutes who were on hand in case that anything went wrong. The windows were then closed and the steam turned on. There was a sign up saying that no one could smoke, but you couldn't help it. You were lucky if you didn't burst into flames.

Nine-thirty! The program begins! Mr. Carlin, the announcer, steps to the "mike" and says: "Good evening, everybody! We are going to listen tonight to Mr. Robert Benchley who—" And you can just hear radio machines from Maine to California being shut off. There were probably more people tuning in on weather reports that night than at any other time in radio history.

However, there is no backing out now and Grandpa steps to the machine. He has his little piece all fixed up, but it suddenly doesn't seem so good. The first wise-crack is pulled into silence. When you are working on a stage, at least you can hear yourself getting the razzberry. On the radio you feel as if you were saying it into Grant's Tomb after he had been taken out. The second wise-crack, and an even worse silence. Grandpa looks around to see if maybe the orchestra isn't laughing. The banjo player is puttering with a hang-nail. The drummer and the flute player are working on a problem of tick-tack-toe. The leader is looking out the window and dreaming of the days when he thought he was going to be a drum-major.

However, there is no backing out now and Grandpa steps to the machine. He has his little piece all fixed up, but it suddenly doesn't seem so good.

And here are you, broken-hearted, and wondering what it's all about.

The funny thing about wise-cracks is that, if you don't get any reaction, they cease being wise-cracks, even to you. The funniest line in the world (which I would like to think up some day but never seem to), if spoken into a vacuum, would sound like the biggest flop in the world. But that is a psychological feature which needs elaboration and this is no place for elaboration. The only thing that can be said here is that if nobody laughs, it isn't funny, that's all.

This goes on for fifteen minutes. All there is in the room is the sound of your own voice, which suddenly becomes the most revolting sound you have ever heard. In the middle of my little act, it was necessary for the male quartet to step up and break the silence with a song. This gave me my chance. I grabbed my hat and said to Mr. Carlin: "Well, I'll be off! See you later." Mr. Carlin said that I was still expected to do more after the quartet stopped. I asked him to do it. "Tell them anything," I said; "tell them that I got a telephone call that my little boy has been arrested. Tell them I have fainted. I'm going!"

But the quartet had stopped and I was "on the air" again. Five more minutes of silent prayer

I rode away into the night. My radio career was at an end.

and the act was over. Jumping on my horse, which I had left saddled and bridled at the door, I rode away into the night. My radio career was at an end.

Ever since then I have been getting letters from Montgomery, Alabama, and Wichita, Kansas, giving answers to some riddles I had asked. I happened to say in the course of my talk that I had lost my hat at the Harvard-Yale game and that if any of my radio audience knew where it was I would appreciate their letting me know. To date, I have received six old hats, C.O.D., seventeen telegrams saying that my hat was in New Rochelle, St. Louis, and Buffalo, and four proposals of marriage. My mother, who heard the thing from Worcester, Mass., called up that night and asked if I had a cold and was I taking good care of myself. My wife and children, who had gathered around the family radio to hear Daddy make a fool of himself, couldn't get the radio to work and heard only an *SOS* from a ship at sea. As a matter of fact, that *SOS* was from Daddy himself. From now on I do my act on a stage in front of people where I can see the vegetables coming in time to dodge.

FASCINATING CRIMES

5—The Strange Case of the Vermont Judiciary

RESIDENTS of Water Street, Bellows Falls (Vt.), are not naturally sound sleepers, owing to the proximity of the Bellows Falls Light and Power Co. and its attendant thumpings, but fifteen years before the erection of the light-and-power plant there was nothing to disturb the slumbers of Water Streetites, with the possible exception of the bestial activities of Roscoe Erkle. For it was Mr. Erkle's whim to creep up upon people as they slept and, leaping on their chests, to cram poisoned biscuits into their mouths until they died, either from the poison or from choking on the crumbs.

A tolerant citizenry stood this as long as it could decently be expected to, and then had Roscoe Erkle arrested. It is not this phase of his career in which we are interested, however, so much as the remarkable series of events which followed.

His trial began at St. Albans, Franklin County, on Wednesday morning, May 7, 1881. Defending Erkle was an attorney appointed by the Court, Enos J. Wheefer. Mr. Wheefer, being deaf, had not heard the name of his client or he would never have taken the case. He thought for several days that he was defending Roscoe Conkling and had drawn up his case with Conkling in mind.

Atty. Herbert J. McNell represented the State and, as it later turned out, a tragic fate gave the case into the hands of Judge Alonso Presty for hearing.

Judge Presty was one of the leaders of the Vermont bar at the time and a man of impeccable habits. It was recalled after his untimely death that he had been something of a rounder in his day, having been a leader in barn-dancing circles while in law school, but since donning the sock and buskin his conduct had been propriety itself. Which makes the events that we are about to relate all the more puzzling.

On the opening day of the trial, Atty. McNell was submitting as evidence passages from the prisoner's diary which indicated that the murders were not only premeditated but a source of considerable delight to Mr. Erkle. It might perhaps be interesting to give a sample page from the diary:

"*Oct.* 7—Cool and fair. Sharp tinge of Fall in the air. New shipment of arsenic arrived from W. Spent all day powdering biscuits and then toasting them. Look good enough to eat.

"*Oct.* 8—Raw, with N. E. wind. Betsy came in

for a minute and we did anagrams. (EDITOR'S
NOTE: *Betsy was Erkle's cow.*)

"*Oct.* 9—Still raw. Cleaned up Water Street on
the left-hand side, with the exception of old Wass-
ner who just wouldn't open his mouth. Home and
read till after midnight. That man Carlyle certainly had the dope on the French Revolution, all
right, all right."

As Atty. McNell read these excerpts from the
diary in a droning voice, the breath of Vermont
May-time wafted in at the open windows of the
courtroom. Now and then a bee hummed in and
out, as if to say: "Buz-z-z-z-z-z!" Judge Presty
sat high above the throng, head resting on his hand,
to all intents and purposes asleep.

Suddenly the attorney for the defendant arose and
said: "I protest, Your Honor. I can not hear what
my learned colleague is saying, but I don't like his
expression!"

There was silence while all eyes turned on the
Judge. But the Judge did not move. Thinking
that he had fallen asleep, as was his custom during
the May term, the attorneys went on. It was not
until he had gradually slipped forward into the
glass of water which stood before him on his desk
that it was discovered that he was dead!

The trial was immediately halted and an investigation begun. Nothing could be discovered about the Judge's person which would give a clue to his mysterious lapse except a tiny red spot just behind his right ear. This, however, was laid to indigestion and the Judge was buried.

Another trial was called for October 10, again in St. Albans. This time Judge Walter M. Bondy was presiding, and the same two attorneys opposed each other. Roscoe Erkle had, during the summer, raised a red beard and looked charming.

On the second day of the trial, while Atty. McNell was reading the prisoner's diary, Judge Bondy passed away quietly at his bench, with the same little red spot behind his right ear that had characterized the cadaver of his predecessor. The trial was again halted, and a new one set for the following May.

By this time, the matter had become one for serious concern. Erkle was questioned, but his only reply was: "Let them mind their own business, then." He had now begun to put pomade on his beard and had it parted in the middle, and, as a result, had married one of the richest spinsters in that section of Vermont.

We need not go into the reptitious account of the succeeding trials. Suffice it to say that the following May Judge Rapf died at his post, the following

October Judge Orsenigal, the May following that a
Judge O'Heel, who had been imported from New
Hampshire without being told the history of the
case, and the succeeding solstices saw the mysterious
deaths of Judges Wheefer (the counsel for the de-
fense in the first trial, who had, in the meantime,
been appointed Judge because of his deafness),
Rossberg, Whelan, Rock, and Brady. And, in each
case, the little telltale mark behind the ear.

The State then decided to rest its case and de-
clare it *nol-prossed*. Judges were not so plentiful
in Vermont that they could afford to go on at this
rate. Erkle was released on his own recognizance,
took up the study of law, and is, at latest accounts,
a well-to-do patent attorney in Oldham. Every
May and every October he reports at St. Albans
to see if they want to try him again, but the Court
laughingly postpones the case until the next term,
holding its hand over its right ear the while.

THE PROBLEM OF THE USED CAR

WITH the introduction of the new Ford car the problem of the used car becomes a national menace comparable only with the old plague of the seven-year locusts. It was bad enough before—as what wasn't?

For years, automobile manufacturers have been confronted with the problem of what to do with the second-hand cars turned in for new ones. The fact that they have given any money at all on second-hand cars shows what a public-spirited crowd the manufacturers are. It is like giving money for the return of water on the knee. When they get their old cars back, what are they to do with them? They can't eat them—that is, not unless they have been boiled down to practically nothing.

Some one has suggested that they be filled with potted plants and used to decorate the public parks, or stuffed with almond meats and used as favors. There is no sense in discussing these solutions. They are obviously too silly. However, we may come back to them if we can't think of something else.

Certain it is that there are a great many more used cars than there are used drivers. A dealer in the Middle West had so many used cars out behind his garage that he closed his house and brought his family down to live in the cars—one car for the living-room, one for the dining-room and, without mentioning any names, one for brushing the children's teeth in. The only trouble was that the smaller children kept falling off the running-boards and hurting themselves and it was difficult getting the winter's coal into the car used for the cellar. The coal men had to toss it in, piece by piece.

Of course, the dealers sooner or later send the used cars back to the factory, but that just puts the problem off on the factory. A factory is supposed to make cars—not serve as a Bide-A-Wee Home for them. Several factories have had to suspend operations on new cars altogether in order to make room for the old ones. This was perhaps overdoing the sentimental phase of the thing a bit, but with the growing tendency toward sentimentality and service in business we are going to find more and more manufacturers who just haven't the heart to turn old cars out on the street when they come straggling home.

The sentimental side of a second-hand car is one which has never been brought out sufficiently. It is not so much the wear and tear which a car has been subjected to during its years of service that makes it difficult to dispose of it. It is the ghosts and memories of former owners which infest its curtains and cushions and make it a veritable haunted house of old associations. I have had dealers tell me that on a still moonlight night they can hardly sleep because of the whistling and clanking which go on among the old cars behind the garage, spirits of Christmas Past and Summer Vacations of years gone by, which flit in and out of the sedans and roadsters, making night hideous for people in the vicinity.

One dealer, braver than the rest, went out one night and poked around among the used cars to see where the noise was coming from. He found nothing.

Several manufacturers have asked me: "What are we to do, Bob?" And my answer always has been: "What would Lincoln have done? (Not the Lincoln Company—the other Lincoln.) You manufacturers are confronted by one of the big problems of the age. Let's sit down and talk this thing over sanely, as one man to another."

And when we sit down, we always come back to the suggestion, discarded earlier in this study of the situation, that the used cars be stuffed with almond meats and used for favors. But then, a lot of people don't like almonds.

CHECKING UP

THE newspapers may not be very frightened of the movie news-reels as competitors in the actual business sense, but they had better watch them pretty closely as rivals in the accurate dispensing of news. A good news-reel can show up a news-story and make it look awfully silly.

An example comes to hand (as a matter of fact, it has been at hand for some weeks) in the visit of President Coolidge to Havana. Naturally this was counted as one of the big maneuvers in the Good Will Campaign which has been under way between this country and the Pan-American republics, or rather which has been aimed *at* the Pan-American republics by this country. The idea was that President Coolidge should go down there and by his cheery manner and hail-fellow-well-met spirit so charm the Cubans that they would forget certain little matters of import and export and just feel as if they were members of One Big Family.

To this end, the reporters who covered the Coolidge Flying Wedge into the hearts of the Cubans did their best. They sent back stories telling of the affectionate enthusiasm with which the Great White Father was received in Havana. They told of the cheers which rolled up from the populace in greeting, of the wild excitement which prevailed as the executive cortège rolled through the streets, of the spirit of friendliness toward the United States which the visit was breeding on every side. One got the impression that Havana went Coolidge-mad.

The next day the Movietone news-reels appeared showing the same procession through the streets of Havana. Not only the visual image of this impressive pageant was offered to public view, but the sounds incident to its passage were recorded as well. And there was a strange discrepancy between the newspaper accounts and this irrefutable testimony of the senses.

For in the Movietone we saw the crowds lining the streets and the Presidential automobile rolling slowly along the avenue, but the enthusiasm was nominal. Here and there some apathetic Cuban would raise his hand in an abortive salute and say, in a voice slightly above the conversational tone, "Americano!" Now and again a hat would be tipped, but whether it was to keep it from being blown off in the wind or to indicate extreme enthusiasm could not be detected. But, for the most part, the entire route might have been that of a particularly unimpressive funeral, let us say of a rear-admiral lately in charge of an inland arsenal. If there was wild excitement such as the newspaper-reporters saw, it must have been in the parlor of the residence of President Machado. If the populace of Havana went wild over President Coolidge it must have been by means of letters to the local papers. Here, before our very eyes, was this triumphant cavalcade we had read so much about, and the only sounds came from the explosions of the motor-cycles of the escort, the only agitation from the breeze as it blew the property flags. Even President Coolidge himself seemed subdued, his gay buoyancy gone, his boyish abandon stilled under the lethargy of his reception.

So the newspapers have got to watch their step from now on. They are being checked up. In the future, as the Movietone principle is developed, they will have to be careful how they tell of Red riots, for the next day the public may have a chance to see and hear that sixteen people merely stood still and hummed the "Internationale" while traffic swirled unconcernedly past. They will have to be careful how they tell of apathetic rebuffs of opposition politicians, for it may turn out in the Movietone account that the audience gave every indication of being excited. In short, news-stories will have to be written pretty much without personal coloring on the part of the reporter, for there will be a dark man coming with a bundle of film right behind him to refute his testimony if it be phoney. All of which may result in the press eventually giving itself over to the publication of comic strips and actual baseball scores.

A SHORT (WHAT THERE IS OF IT) HISTORY OF AMERICAN POLITICAL PROBLEMS

CHAP. I VOL. I.

IN our two introductions to this history (one of which was lost) we made a general survey of the development of political theory and practice from Plato down to Old Man ("He Must Know Nothin'") River. In beginning our history proper, it might perhaps be wise to forget all that we have said before and start fresh, as a lot of new things have come up since the last introduction was written (such as the Abolition of Slavery and the entire Reconstruction Period) which have changed the political aspect considerably.

We will begin our history, therefore, with the year 1800; in the first place, because 1800 is a good round number and easily remembered (Vanderbilt 1800, for instance), and in the second place, because it marked the defeat of the Federalist Party under Hamilton by the Republicans under Jefferson.

Now you are going to start back in astonishment

138

when I say "Republicans under Jefferson" and most likely will write in and say, "What do you mean, *Republicans* under Jefferson, you big old gump you! Everybody knows that it was Jefferson who founded the *Democratic* Party. . . . Yours truly (whatever your name happens to be). . . .

And here is where I will have the laugh on you, because you will have forgotten what I told you in one of our introductions to this history about the present Democratic Party having once been called the Republican Party. So when I say "Republicans under Jefferson" I *mean* "Republicans under Jefferson" and no more back talk out of you, either. If you had devoted half the time to reading one, or both, of the introductions to this history that you devote to jazz and petting-parties you would know something about the political history of your country instead of being such a nimcompoop. (There was a political party named the "Nimcompoops" a little later on, and I can hardly wait to tell you about it. . . . Perhaps I won't wait. I may tell about it any minute now. [Adv.])

Now the reason for the defeat of the Federalists in 1800 was based on several influences which have a rather important bearing on our story. They were:

1. The Federalists (as I have told you again and

again until I am sick of it) thought that the Federal Government ought to have the power to rule the various states with a rod of iron. A good way to remember this is by means of an old rhyme: "The Federalists thought that the Federal Government ought to have the power to rule the various states with a rod of iron. Rum-tiddy-um-tum-tum-tiron!"

2. Hamilton himself was very snooty.

3. Adams (John), the Federalist President, was very snooty and a Harvard man into the bargain.

4. No one ever had any fun.

Jefferson, on the other hand, believed that the various states ought to be allowed to govern themselves, using the Federal Government only when company came or when there was a big reception or something. This appealed to the various states, and as, after all, the various states were made up of the voters themselves and the Federal Government consisted chiefly of Hamilton and Adams and their families, it is little wonder that, on a majority vote, the various states won.

So, in 1801, Thomas Jefferson took over the reins of the government and the Republican Party had its first opportunity to show the strength of its principles.

But we are getting ahead of our story.

In our next chapter we will take up the final collapse of the Federalists and the appearance of the Whigs. There will also be dancing and a brief reaffirmation of America's debt of gratitude to France.

CEASE FIRING!

THERE are signs that the direct frontal attack on Babbittry, maintained so pitilessly and monotonously by the writing forces for ten years, has reached its peak and is about to recede. This will be a relief to many people, including the Babbitts and the Public. It has been a cruel assault, from which the Go-Getter has emerged both bloody and bowed, as witness the fact that he has now taken to kidding himself in nervous apprehension. His only chance for an honorable peace is that unstrategic ones among the writers will continue the mauling to a point where reaction sets in and the Babbitt becomes a public hero. This point has almost been reached.

But before we blame the literati for harping too continuously on the Go-Getter's little weaknesses, we must think back a couple of decades and remember what inspired this spirit of blind vindictiveness. It could not have come seething as it does from the writer's soul without some preliminary period of stewing. And, as a belligerent scrivener who recalls the day when the Business Man was in the saddle, lashing down us poor peasants as we stood in the market-place begging for bread, I am almost in a mood to rally my comrades about for another and more sanguinary assault, this time perpetrating nameless horrors.

For there was a time, not so long ago as the crow-eater flies, when the man who wrote for his living was the butt for jokes around the very conference-table which he now throws pop-bottles at. There was a time when anyone who made his living by writing was an impractical sap, gifted along certain lines perhaps, but lines which led nowhere and contributed nothing to the State. If he was spoken to at all by the geniuses of business and organization, it was with fine scorn and in words of two syllables. "Herbert is a nice fellow," they would say among themselves, "but he writes."

Perhaps the young writer's first realization that he was a pariah and a drag on the wheels of Progress came when he was in school or college and a member of the literary staff of his college paper. Here it was the "Business End" which dominated. The Business End held the Writing End in jesting contempt and made no effort to conceal it. "Where would the paper be," they asked (and with just enough justice to lend authority), "where would the paper be if it were not for the ads?" And the Writing End cowered in its sanctum and scratched with its pens in an attempt to placate the Business End and perhaps get a kind word from them at the finish of the term.

I have no doubt but that the venom of Sinclair Lewis, commander-in-chief of the Anti-Babbitt forces, was brewed while in college. He probably heard some man on the Business End say, as every young scrivener of that period heard said of himself: "Oh, yes, Lewis is a nice enough fellow—but he writes, you know." The feeling was that if a man wrote, certain sections of his brain were atrophied and that it was those brain-cells, in the normal man, which made for keenness, virility and desirability as a citizen of the greatest country in the world.

From college the embryo writers of twenty years ago went out into a world where they were even more of a laughing-stock than they had been under the academic elms. If they went into business they were forced to take seriously all the talk they heard about "organization," "efficiency," "service" and "distribution," or they were fired. They listened to men who were obviously charlatans tell them that they were half-witted and incompetent if they scribbled on their conference-pads some slight heresy against the hokum of Business. They were knocked about from one corner of the office to another by officials whose own jobs depended on their ability to conceal what they didn't know and if, by any chance, they wrote something on the side which happened to be published, they were brought up on the soft green carpet and told to stop fooling around or they would never get anywhere in this organization. Without knowing anything about the facts in the case, I suspect that Sinclair Lewis' first gun in his memorable charge against the Go-Getter ("Our Mr. Wrenn") was the result of several nasty wounds received at the hands of the advertising moguls of the day.

And if the young writer of the first decade of the century went directly into literature, he might just as well have donned the cap and bells and gone out on the street corner for all the respect he had in the offices and manufacturing plants of the country. Some of them even took pseudonyms to hide their disgrace. One, who later became one of the most successful short story writers of the day, wrote under the name of "Holworthy Hall" because he felt that, to use his own name, would be fatal to his chances in the advertising firm with which he was connected. Writing was a thing to be done on the sly unless you wanted to be known as unreliable in the more serious branches of human activity.

But scarcely had the report of "Our Mr. Wrenn" echoed around a very small world when several hundred worms began to turn uneasily. Abortive blows were struck at the idols in the temple. They did no more than chip off a nose-tip or so, but they gave the poor ink-stained wretches courage. A barrage was on which was to gather momentum in the next few years until it became deafening. And behold, the enemy was yellow! At first, the Go-Getter maintained a scornful silence, but not for long. And his first move was not in defiance. It was to duck. As the attack increased in intensity, rising to its full volume in Mr. Lewis' "Babbitt," he closed his ears and ran to cover. Book after book kidding Business and Business-men was hurled at him; magazine articles were printed by hundreds over the weak protests of the once-domineering Business End; even the comic weeklies took up the assault, and the words "babbitt," "go-getter" and "efficiency expert" became a part of the satirical language of the nation. Even the babbitts themselves, at their Rotary luncheons, tried to disassociate themselves from their tribe and kid other babbitts, just as one of two drunken men tries to give the impression that he knows how bad his companion is and is there only to help him home. Never did a down-trodden rabble rise up in such might as the impractical scribes, and never has there been such a complete rout of the reigning princes.

But, as is always the case in a revolution, the rebels have outdone themselves. They have not only driven the royal family out of the palace, but they are sacking and burning. They are running through the streets with flaming torches, trying to destroy everything that bears the hated coat-of-arms. In the first place, the reading public is getting a little sick of pseudo-satirical cracks at Big Business. In the second place, the writers are donning the purple robes of Big Business themselves and are turning into babbitts. Unless a halt is called soon, a counter-revolution will be organized and the writers themselves shot against the wall. (I have several names which I will drop into the lion's mouth when the time comes.) The victory has been won. The writers should accept their laurels and go home. But it should never be forgotten that what they did they did under the direst provocation that an oppressed people ever had. Next time let the ruling classes think twice.

THE GREAT AMERICAN FOLLY

I T IS funny that going over Niagara Falls in a barrel never achieved more popularity in this country as a method of taking a trip. You would think that it would appeal to Americans to such an extent as to make it necessary to run excursion barrels over the Falls during July and August. For, as a nation, we seem to be more gluttonous for punishment in respect to uncomfortable traveling than any nation on earth. Witness the number of people who take train trips in the summer—for *pleasure*.

Here is a great nation confronted each summer with the problem of vacationing. Almost every locality has some spot within walking distance where a very passable vacation could be spent. But no! We must pack trunks and bags and go somewhere too far away even to motor, just so that we can go choo-choo during the hottest months of the year—or of any year, for that matter.

A foreigner visiting this country during a torrid spell and seeing the great terminals crowded with moist, bedraggled travelers, snapping at each other and pinching their children's arms to keep them in line, would surely think that nothing short of a great catastrophe or enemy invasion could set so many people on the march in such weather. And then next day he reads in the papers that "Record Crowd of Holiday-Makers Throng Terminals." Holiday-makers! A Roman holiday, such as Nero might have planned.

With the advent of the hot weather, your American citizen begins to get restless and to look up time tables. He finds that he can leave Cleveland at six and get into Dallas at four-fifty or that he can leave Boston at noon and get into Los Angeles at nine-twenty. Of course, the railroads can't predict for him just what the hottest day of the month will be, but he has a fine instinct for picking it in advance. If he could pick horses or stocks with the same sagacity that he picks hot days for traveling, there would be less poverty in this country and fewer overdrafts.

If, by any chance, he hasn't got his ticket in advance, he waits until some evening the sun sets very round and red and all the natives say, "A hot day tomorrow, brother!" and then he rushes home and throws a few things into a bag, gets all his children (if he hasn't children, he borrows some from a neighbor) and sets his alarm for six in order to be up with the blistering sun and off on the 8:45 for a two-day cinder bath.

Probably one of the most depressing sights in the world is a family entering a train drawing room on a good steamy morning, all ready for a trip across the continent or as far as their money will take them. Their train has been frying in the yards all the day before and all night and as they all push their way into the little box they are to call "home" for two days, Mother and one of the frailer daughters faint immediately.

"Well, well," says Daddy, cheerily, "it's going to be a scorcher all right," and to hear him you might think that it was all his doing. The bags are put in the racks and piled up behind the door, Mother and the frailer daughter are brought to temporarily, Daddy takes off his coat and sits in that good American hot-weather institution, the woolen waistcoat, and everything is set.

Someone thinks of turning on the fan. This is a Pullman contrivance whereby heated air from the engine is brought through asbestos pipes and set in motion in the drawing rooms. Its effect is that of a soft sponge of chloroform held close against the nose. At the first whirl of the fan, out goes Mother again.

As the train starts, everyone crowds to the window to get whatever air there may be, and that is a good joke, too, for there isn't any air. There is

"Well, well," says Daddy cheerily, "it's going to be a scorcher
all right."

something on which the soot travels, but it isn't air. Something for physicists to discover some day is what that element is that comes in at train windows in summer. It might be turned to some good use if it could only be isolated and harnessed, such as frying wheatcakes or popping corn, for instance.

Now all this would be very terrible if this family had *had* to make the trip at this particular time. It would be wrong for us to laugh at other people's sufferings. But this is the result of months of careful planning and eager anticipation. Everybody knows what trains are in late June, July, and August, and that is evidently why everybody takes trains in late June, July, and August rather than at any other time.

If any one factor more than another is making for the gradual disintegration of the American family and the increase of divorce it is this custom of family traveling in summer. I saw a family of four leaving Chicago last summer on the way to the Coast. They had two drawing rooms and seemed to be the best of friends when the train pulled out of the Santa Fe station. (May I explain that I was taking the trip on *business?* When I want a vacation I get in a rowboat.) The next morning it was 98 in Kansas City and the sun wasn't up yet. By Emporia it was 105. The family in question were my next-door neighbors and gradually I began to hear voices being raised in querulous bickering. There seemed to be some argument as to whether they should have lunch brought in to them or go into the diner.

"It can't be any worse in the diner than it is in here," someone said.

"Oh, it can't, can't it? Have you ever *been* in a diner?"

"Yes, I've been in a diner and I know what I'm talking about."

"If you didn't have all those things hanging up on the hooks it would be a little cooler in here."

"*My* things! Two-thirds of them are yours."

Then there was a sound of things being yanked off hooks and packed into a suitcase.

"*Now*—I suppose you are cooler! Now I guess you'll need an overcoat."

"Well, at any rate, the air gets a chance to circulate."

"*Air!* What air?"

This went on, sometimes louder, sometimes softer, according to the stamina of the speaker. Finally two of them went into the diner and two of them had lunch served in the drawing room. None of them ate anything; just sat around and gasped.

This went on all across Kansas, and during the

night there were sounds of restless banging and murmured threats. At Albuquerque the next afternoon, one member of the family got off and took the next train back, another got off and bought a house in Albuquerque and I guess is living there yet. The other two continued on to the Coast but in separate drawing rooms and didn't speak to each other again. One of them was carried off on a stretcher at Pasadena.

This sort of thing is going on every summer in almost every train going in almost any direction. Is it any wonder that our people are becoming loosely knit.

Of course, the phenomenon of railroad excursions in summer is even more startling. In every railroad station in the country you will see great posters advertising cut-rate excursions for the Fourth of July. The one day in the year when anyone with any brains would plan to get into the bath tub with a good book and pull down the shades is the one day in the year when the citizenry put on stiff collars and take a round trip to Savannah, Georgia, Washington, D. C., or Old Point Comfort. And a round trip at that! None of this staying and. getting a bath anywhere. Just jam on the train and sit in the heat until you get some place—and then jam on the train and sit in the heat until you get back. I don't know what to make of it.

Perhaps the explanation is that some of the people are crazy some of the time; some of the people are crazy all of the time, and in late June, July, and August all of the people are crazy all of the time.

JUNIOR DRAMA

Latitude 41.54 N.
Longitude 58.27 W.

THE dramatic season on the French Line opened this afternoon at three sharp with a performance in the *Guignol,* or, as you Americans say, the "Punch and Judy." It was held in the Children's Room and was a gala affair, except for one little girl who was badly frightened and had to be led out. She was much too young to have been brought, anyway, and it is to be hoped that the *Guignol* season will not receive a black eye around the ship because of this one small critic who left early.

The French give themselves much more latitude in their Punch and Judy (as they do in so many other of life's pleasures) and do not feel obliged to stick to the old plot every time. In fact, *Punch* and *Judy* as characters did not appear on the opening bill at all. The only familiar touch was the hanging at the end, doubtless put in as a concession to public sentimentality.

The bill consisted of two pieces—one a curtain raiser called *"La bonne Chance de M. Mouton,"* and the other a realistic crime melodrama entitled *"Le*

Voleur" (not the Bernstein piece recently revived by Alice Brady). Both plays were strictly original and dealt with two of the more sordid phases of life in Paris. One might almost object to them on the ground that, while such low characters undoubtedly do exist in real life, they are not what one goes to the theatre to see. However, this department has never been one to cavil at the theme of a play and we do not intend to begin caviling now, at least not in mid-ocean.

The first piece, *"La bonne Chance de M. Mouton,"* hardly calls for extended comment. It was received with marked indifference by the first afternoon audience, as it deserved to be. What seemed like hours of expository dialogue between *M. Mouton* and a character who appeared to be a Chinaman of some sort thoroughly bored the spectators and there was a great deal of fidgeting among the younger members of the audience (those between three and four) and practically a running fire of high treble conversation with nurses and parents. It was not until *M. Mouton* (played with little or no distinction by the largest puppet of the troupe) began beating his wife that the audience showed signs of following the plot at all.

This sudden sadistic streak in *M. Mouton* came as quite a surprise, as he had seemed entirely devoted to dialectics up to this point, besides being a man well along in his seventies. But evidently *Mme. Mouton* was of a type which irritated him, for he beat her into insensibility and threw her out behind the house for no particular reason. We are sorry to report that this brutality pleased the audience enormously, and that there were loud demands for more.

In *"Le Voleur"* (in free translation, "The Thief") we find more of that gaiety which one associates with the French, although here, too, we should say that the French puppets hit each other much harder than is necessary and display a viciousness in belaboring a victim after he is obviously unconscious which detracts a little from the light-heartedness of the comedy.

The plot of *"Le Voleur"* is soon told—if at all. A lady keeps placing articles of furniture out on the sidewalk in front of her house (either the reason for this is not brought out in the dialogue or our French is not what it was), only to have each article in succession stolen by a mean-looking man as soon as she goes back into the house for more. A piano, a table, a dish-cabinet, and finally a bed are thus taken right under her very eyes, and a gendarme who is called in each time proves to be worse than useless, owing to drink. The whole thing up to this

The chairs are awfully low for a six-foot spectator.

point is very improbable, but it drew down screams of laughter from the audience and so justifies itself on the ground of being what the public wants.

The thief is finally apprehended through trickery (we were asked not to divulge the plot), and is beaten in good old French fashion until his head hangs limp over the edge of the stage-apron, after which he is given a couple more socks for good measure. Then, to make doubly sure that he will menace society no longer, he is hanged from a gallows and the magistrate and gendarme dance away, with him in a coffin, singing *"Auprès de ma Blonde."*

We have gone into this plot at length because it seems to indicate a tendency on the part of the French to follow the Eugene O'Neill influence in cumulative tragedy. Not one piece of furniture is stolen, but four, each one larger than the last. Not one sock on the nose is given, but eight. The protagonist of the drama is not only killed by beating—he is hanged as well. It is Life closing in on him. It is Truth and Beauty.

Incidentally, we should like to complain of just one thing in the Children's Room equipment. The chairs are awfully low for a six-foot spectator, and tip over too easily when the ship rolls.

THE PASSING OF THE COW

(With Wild West Sketches from the Author's Notebook)

ONE of the signs of the gradual deterioration of the West is the even more gradual disappearance of the cow. By "cow" is meant any heavy animal that lumbers along mooing, regardless of sex. There has been too much attention paid to sex lately.

According to the startling statistics of the U. S. Cow-Counting Bureau issued on Monday (for release Wednesday), there are not more than six or seven real cows left in the West. This, at first blush, would seem to be an understatement when one thinks of the number of animals that *look* like cows that one sees from the back of the prairie-schooner as one drives across the plains. But certainly the U. S. Cow-Counting Bureau ought to know a cow when it sees one. These other animals must be impostors.

Accepting these statistics—or this statistic—as genuine, we find ourselves confronted by a pretty

161

serious situation. The cow has been called "Man's best friend." No, that is the dog. . . . Sorry.

The situation is serious, regardless of who Man's

Horse and Rider.

(If I were doing this over again, I would put a large cactus in to hide the horse's front legs. And maybe his hind ones, too. Perhaps I would just have the cowboy standing there.)

best friend is. Without cows (and if, when these figures were compiled, there were only six or seven left in the West, it is safe to assume that even these are gone by now) things look pretty black. It sometimes seems as if it were hardly worth while going on.

Ever since 1847 the cow has been the feature of the West that most appealed to the imagination. Prior to 1847 it was thought that all these animals were horses. You can imagine the surprise of the man who first discovered otherwise.

One of the steers that has disappeared.

(This is easily the worst drawing of the lot. It has, however, caught something of the spirit of the old West.)

With the discovery of cows came the cowboy. And with the cowboy came the moving picture. So you see!

It is related, in an old cowboy ballad, how the first cow was lassoed. It seems that Ernest Guilfoil, known as "Mr. Ernest Guilfoil," was practicing swinging his rope one day, trying to synchronize gum-chewing with rope-twirling so that he could work in a monologue between the two and go on the stage. He had the gum-chewing and monologue all synchronized, but was having trouble with the rope. Suddenly, after a particularly complicated session

Cowboy chasing cow.

(It has never been very easy for me to draw animals, and it seems to be getting harder and harder as I grow older. For instance, that cow is not right and I know it. The horse is a little better, but seems to have too much personality. At any rate, the etching has action. Perhaps it would have been better to write an article just about cowboys themselves.)

with the "pesky" thing, he felt a tug on the other end and, on reeling it in, discovered that he had entangled a cow in the noose. Terrified, he jumped on his pony and rode to the nearest corral, dragging the luckless cow behind him. Thus "Mr. Ernest Guilfoil" became the first cowboy.

The first inkling that the world at large had of the lack of cows was the concentration of cowboys in rodeos and Wild West shows. Here it was possible for a dozen or so cowboys to work on one cow, using the same one over and over at each performance. But it was not until the Bureau of Cow-Counting made its staggering analysis that the public finally realized what had happened. And now it is too late. Just what is to be done about it is a problem. Some suggest moving a lot of cows on from the East, but old-time Westerners feel that this would be adding insult to injury. The alternative seems to be to bring the cowboys on to where the cows are, but that wouldn't work out either, because—oh, because it *wouldn't*, that's all.

And so it comes about that romance dies and Civilization charges ahead. But some of us are wondering, "Is it all worth it?"

BACK TO THE GAME

THIS is about the time of year (it would be a good joke on me if this chapter were held over until Spring) when the old boys begin thinking of going back to college to the Big Game. All during the year they have never given a thought to whether they were alumni of Yale or the New York Pharmaceutical College, but as soon as the sporting pages begin telling about O'Brienstein of Harvard and what a wonderful back he is, all Harvard men with cigar-ashes on their waistcoats suddenly remember that they went to Harvard and send in their applications for the Yale Game. There is nothing like a college education to broaden a man.

Going back to the old college town is something of an ordeal, in case you want to know. You think it's going to be all right and you have a little dream-picture of how glad the boys will be to see you. "Weekins, 1914" you will say, and there will be a big demonstration, with fire-works and retchings. The word will go around that Weekins, 1914, is back and professors in everything but Greek will say to their classes: "Dismissed for the day, gentle-

men. Weekins, 1914, is back!" And a happy
crowd of boys will rush pell-mell out of the recita-
tion-hall and down to the Inn to take the horses

A couple of young men come in and, seeing you, go right out
again.

from your carriage (or put horses into it) and drag
you all around the Campus. (My using the word
"Campus" is just a concession to the rabble. Where
I come from "Campus" is a place where stage-

collegians in skull-caps romp around and sing "When Love Is Young in Springtime" in four-part harmony. The reservation in question is known as "the Yard," and I will thank you to call it that in future.)

Anyone who has ever gone back to the old college town after, let us say, ten years, will realize that this country is going to the dogs, especially as regards its youth in the colleges. You get your tickets for the Big Game and you spend a lot of money on railroad fare. (That's all right; you have made a lot of money since getting out. You can afford it.) When you get to the old railroad station you can at least expect that Eddie, the hack-driver, will remember you. Eddie, however, is now pretty fat and has five men working for him. You can't even get one of his cabs, much less a nod out of him. "O. K. Eddie! The hell with you!"

You go to the fraternity house (another concession on my part to my Middle West readers) and announce yourself as "Weekins, 1914." (My class was 1912, as a matter of fact. I am giving myself a slight break and trying to be mysterious about this whole thing.) A lone Junior who is hanging around in the front room says "How do you do? Come on in," and excuses himself immediately. The old place looks about the same, except that an odd-looking banner on the wall says "1930," there being no such year. A couple of young men come in and, seeing you, go right out again. Welcome back to the old House, Weekins!

A steward of some sort enters the room and arranges the magazines on the table.

"Rather quiet for the day of the Big Game," you say to him. "Where is everybody?"

This frightens him and he says: "Thank you, sir!" and also disappears.

Well, after all, you *do* have a certain claim on this place. You helped raise the money for the mission furniture and somewhere up on the wall is a stein with your name on it. There is no reason why you should feel like an intruder. This gives you courage to meet the three young men who enter with books under their arms and pass right by into the hall.

"My name is Weekins, 1914," you say. "Where is everybody?"

"Classes are just over," one of them explains. "Make yourself at home. My name is Hammerbiddle, 1931."

Somehow the mention of such a year as "1931" enrages you. "1931 what? Electrons?" But the three young men have gone down the hall; so you will never know.

A familiar face!   In between the bead portières comes a man, bald and fat, yet with something about him that strikes an old G chord.

"Billigs!" you cry.

"Stanpfer is the name," he says. "Think of seeing you here!"

You try to make believe that you knew that it was Stanpfer all the time and were just saying Billigs to be funny.

"It must be fifteen years," you say.

"Well, not quite," says Stanpfer, "I saw you two years ago in New York."

"Oh, yes, I know, *that!*"   (Where the hell did you see him two years ago?   The man is crazy.) "But I mean it must be fifteen years since we were here together."

"Fourteen," he corrects.

"I guess you're right.   Fourteen.   Well, how the hell are you?"

"Great!   How are you?"

"Great!   How are you?"

"Great!   Couldn't be better.   Everything going all right?"

"Great!   All right with you?"

"Great!   All right with you?"

"You bet."

"That's fine! Kind of quiet around here."

"That's right! Not much like the old days."

"That's right."

"Yes, sir! That's right!"

Perhaps it would be better if the 1931 boys came back. At least, you wouldn't have to recall old days with them. You could start at scratch. Here comes somebody! Somebody older than you, if such a thing is possible.

"Hello," he says, and falls on his face against the edge of the table, cutting his forehead rather badly.

"Up you get!" you say, suiting the action to the word.

"A very nasty turn there," he says, crossly. "They should have that banked."

"That's right," you agree. You remember him as a Senior who was particularly snooty to you when you were a sophomore.

"My name is Feemer, 1911," he says, dabbing his forehead with his handkerchief.

"Weekins, 1914," you say.

"Stanpfer, 1914," says Billigs.

"I remember you," says Feemer, "you were an awful pratt."

You give a short laugh.

Feemer begins to sing loudly and hits his head

again against the table, this time on purpose. Several of the undergraduates enter and look disapprovingly at all three of you.

By this time Feemer, through constant hitting of his head and lurching about, is slightly ill. The general impression is that you and Stanpfer (or Billigs) are drunk too. These old grads!

The undergraduates (of whom there are now eight or ten) move unpleasantly about the room, rearranging furniture that Feemer has upset and showing in every way at their disposal that they wish you had never come.

"What time is the game?" you ask. You know very well what time the game is.

Nobody answers.

"How are the chances?" Just why you should be making *all* the advances you don't know. After all, you are fourteen years out and these boys could almost be your sons.

"I want everybody here to come to Chicago with me after the game," says Feemer, tying his tie. "I live in Chicago and I want everybody here to come to Chicago with me after the game. I live in Chicago and I want everybody here to come to Chicago with me after the game."

Having made this blanket invitation, Feemer goes to sleep standing up.

The undergraduate disapproval is manifest and includes you and Billigs (or Stanpfer) to such an extent that you might better be at the bottom of the lake.

"How are the chances?" you ask again. "Is Derkwillig going to play?"

"Derkwillig has left college," says one of the undergraduates, scornfully. "He hasn't played since the Penn State game."

"Too bad," you say. "He was good, wasn't he?"

"Not so good."

"I'm sorry. I thought he was, from what I read in the papers."

"The papers are crazy," says a very young man, and immediately leaves the room.

There is a long silence, during which Feemer comes to and looks anxiously into each face as if trying to get his bearings, which is exactly what he is trying to do.

"We might as well clear the room out," says one of the undergraduates. "The girls will be coming pretty soon and we don't want to have it looking messy."

Evidently "looking messy" means the presence of you, Feemer and Stanpfer. This is plain to be seen. So you and Stanpfer each take an arm of Feemer and leave the house. Just as you are going

There is no sign of recognition on either side.

down the steps (a process which includes lurching with Feemer from side to side) you meet Dr. Raddi-well and his wife. There is no sign of recognition on either side.

There is a train leaving town at 1:55. You get it and read about the game in the evening papers.

IT SEEMS THERE WERE A COUPLE
OF CELLS

*T*HE *scene is a plateau of primeval ooze.*
Things are in terrible shape. Nobody knows
what to do because there is nobody. The Earth is
practically new and nothing is alive except a lot
of—what shall we say?

Two of these emerge from the mud together and
sit down on a dry spot. There seems to be some
idea of talking things over.

FIRST UNICELLULAR UNIT: How are you fixed
for insurance?

SECOND UNIT: I don't know. How are you?

FIRST UNIT: That reminds me, I saw Lilith the
other day and she has put on weight.

SECOND UNIT: Where?

FIRST UNIT: Where has she put on weight?

SECOND UNIT: No, no—where did you see her?
I phrased my question clumsily.

FIRST UNIT: I should say you *did!*

SECOND UNIT: Oh, well, what's the diff? Nobody
is perfect.

FIRST UNIT: Is that any reason why we shouldn't

176

each one of us try just as hard as we can to make this little old world a happier place to live in? I, for one, am sick and tired of living a lie.

SECOND UNIT: I know what you mean, of course, but I really think that "lie" is a little too harsh a word.

FIRST UNIT: You certainly are a stickler, Phil, but darned if I don't feel better just for having talked to you. If I could only get rid of this old headache!

SECOND UNIT: Where does it ache—here in front?

FIRST UNIT: No, right here, from the top of my head right over back.

SECOND UNIT: I know all about that kind. Mine usually turn into a regular sick headache and I have to go to bed.

FIRST UNIT: My, my, that's no fun.

SECOND UNIT: Well, I suppose it's back to the old grind. I'd like to take the afternoon off.

FIRST UNIT: Heigh-ho! No such luck!

(*They slip back into the ooze and disappear.*)

NO RESULTS WHATEVER IN OUR OWN
STRAW VOTE

IN summarizing the results of our straw vote
(really *your* straw vote, too, for what's ours is
yours and we don't ever want you to forget that,
dear) we must bear two things in mind: (1) that
Hoover is the Republican candidate and Smith the
Democratic, and (2) that red photographs black.
Any other little things that you can remember will
help, too.

We finally covered the entire nation with our
personal canvass, twenty million odd voters (some
of them odder than others, but all pretty bad), and
it was quite a task, you may be sure. Some nights
we didn't get home until after seven for dinner and
we were so tired that we cried if anyone pointed a
finger at us—especially if they added, "There is
the murderer of Roger Preston!" (For, indeed, we
are the murderer of Roger Preston and we don't care
who knows it. We murdered him because everywhere we went he followed us with those green eyes
of his . . . those horrible green eyes . . . everywhere. . . . We had to kill him. . . . God! can't
you understand?) Results . . . Hoover . . . so

many votes. . . . Smith . . . so many votes. . . .
Rogers . . . so many votes, and such *nice* votes!

From our conversations with voters we are able to
tabulate some trends in popular sentiment and perhaps even make a graph. (O Lord! keep us from
making a joke about Graph Zeppelin!) It is the
result of these tabulations and graphs that we wish
to bring before you tonight. . . . Go on there, get
back into your seat!

In respect of the three leading issues of the campaign, Prohibition, Farm Relief and Water Power,
it was found that the average voter likes Prohibition
best because he knows what the word means. He
doesn't *dis*like Farm Relief and Water Power, mind
you, but he gets them mixed up with the Gold
Standard and Nullification, which aren't issues at all
in this election. All four are more or less grouped
in his mind under the general head of "The Tariff,"
which makes it easier to remember.

But he *knows* Prohibition means that, for every
drink he buys, a certain percentage of the price
must be paid to the Government for protection.
And he likes the idea of this, for your American is
a docile soul and craves paternalism; and the
thought that a benevolent government is watching
over him and protecting him is worth the added
seventy-five cents.

The above paragraph is a little disturbing to us, as it is the first one we have ever written about Prohibition. We wanted to be known as the only hack-writer in America who had not waxed satirical on that subject. That's what taking a straw vote does for you.

. But, to get back to the Hoover-Smith-Rogers contest. The result of our tabulation shows that the chances favor the election of Norman Thomas, the Socialist candidate. Mr. Rogers' promise to resign immediately if elected has made it probable that he will be offered the Honorary Presidency and that Mr. Thomas will receive the actual votes of the people. We base our conclusion on the following figures.

Twelve million voters were found who believed that Hoover wouldn't change things if he were elected. Twelve million five hundred voters were found who believed that Smith wouldn't change things if he were elected. Twenty-four million five hundred voters were found who wanted things changed. Evidently the only candidate who can be counted on to change things (aside from Mr. Rogers) is the Socialist candidate. The only thing that remains now to insure his election is to find out where he is.

This, in a way, brings to an end our canvass of

voters. It is a rather sad occasion, for we have enjoyed every minute of it and feel sure that you have, too. We may have had our little differences of opinion, but it has all been good-natured and if we never see any of you again it will be all right with us.

But before we make our final table of analysis, let us run over again, in review, each of the cases we have cited and see if there isn't some other meaning that can be read into them.

FINAL RESULT OF STRAW VOTE

Number of voters in the
  United States................Millions and millions
Number of voters interviewed.....Really only about six
Result of
  canvass.......Pains in the neck and occasional nausea
Not voting 6

    TOTAL 6

TWO EDITORIALS FOR "THE NATION"

(if it doesn't mind)

INDIA RESURGENT

THERE seems to be some slight misapprehension in the public mind concerning the motives behind the recent anti-British revolt in India, or rather concerning the anti-British revolt which is imminent in India. This is doubtless due to the fact that the situation has been befogged by the statements issued by the British Foreign Office and by the International Wagons-Lits.

There are three distinct parties in India: the Centrist, the Grand Centrist and the Right Wing Under. Sometimes one hears of another party—the Old Party Returning Slightly the Worse for Wear from a Regimental Dinner—but that is only in *Punch,* and is never very funny.

The Centrist Party, or adherents of Rahman Digg, have been in power now for six or seven *yearos,* and have ruled with an iron hand. They have suppressed free speech; they have advocated a seven-cent subway fare; they have been just as nasty as they could be to a whole lot of people. This has been due to the fact that India now functions under an obsolete law known as Ohm's Law, whereby a falling body increases in physical attraction thirty-two feet per second per second, making it, by the time it has landed, practically irresistible.

Against this law there has been a vast amount of agitation on the part of the people who like nice things. The Grand Centrists, or advocates of the Slightly-Ajar Door policy, have taken the middle course, as usual, and are trying to drag a fish, fowl, or good red herring across the trail in order to avoid the issue. Our correspondent, whose article on the subject appears on another page, seems to feel that the issue can not be avoided. We are inclined to agree with him.

The time is coming when England must take India into account, just as there was a time coming when the United States had to take Nicaragua into account and didn't, and when Italy had to take the Tyrol into account and hasn't yet. But, sooner or later, all these things will come to pass, either through revolution or violet rays or that Divine Law which watches over children and drunkards, and when that times comes, it will be time for France to take the French peasant into account and depose that tyrant who now holds court at Versailles.

MR. KELLOGG'S DILEMMA

IT is perhaps not too early to begin worrying about the next Nicaraguan crisis, if the present one can really be said ever to have abated. That the United States has acted in bad faith goes without saying, but even that would not seem to justify Secretary Kellogg's arbitrary destruction of the machine-guns captured on the Austro-Hungarian border. If Mussolini wants an ally against Jugoslavia, and we have every indication that he does, he has at his disposal the counter clock-wise sections of the Treaty of the Trianon, and unless he is definitely and ruthlessly out to make an enemy of the Bratiano government, he can do better than oppose President Leguia (of Peru somewhere). We have as yet had no occasion to change our original opinion that a merger between the Seiyukai, or landed interests of Japan, and the forces of Sandino would not only prove an embarrassment to Secretary Kellogg but would bring the whole matter to a head and confuse the issue to a point where the United States would have to explain its position or "eat crow."

THE FOUR-IN-HAND OUTRAGE

WHAT has happened to four-in-hand ties that they refuse to slide around under the collar any more? Or am I just suffering from a persecution complex?

For maybe ten years I have been devoted to the soft collar or sport model, the polo shirt, and other informal modes in collarings affected by the *jeunesse dorée*. They have not been particularly adapted to playing up my good points in personal appearance, but they are easy to slip into in the morning.

With the approach of portly middle-age, however, and the gradual but relentless assumption of power in the financial world, it seemed to me that I ought to dress the part. When a man goes into a bank to ask to have his note extended he should at least wear a stiff collar and a four-in-hand of some rich, dark material, preferably a foulard. He owes it to himself.

So I laid in a stock of shirts (two) which called for either stiff collars or a knotted bandana, and then set about digging up some collars to go with them. My old stock of "Graywoods 14½" which

185

I have been devoted to informal modes of **Collarings** affected
by the *jeunesse dorée*.

I used to wear in high-school proved useless. They were of the mode, so flashy in those days, which came close together in front, allowing just a tip of the knitted club-tie to peek out from under the corners. And, owing to a temporary increase in neck-size (I can reduce it at any time by dieting for two or three days), 14½ is no longer my number. So I bought several styles of a more modern collar and prepared to throw the world of fashion into a tumult by appearing in formal neckwear on, let us say, the following Wednesday at high noon.

But in the ten years which have elapsed since I last tied a four-in-hand under a stiff collar something perverse has been injected into the manufacture of either the ties or the collars. My male readers will recognize a manœuvre which I can best designate as the Final Tug, the last short pull-around of the tie under the collar before tightening the knot. This, under the present system, has become practically impossible. The tie refuses to budge; I pull and yank, take the collar off and rearrange the tie, try gentle tactics, followed suddenly by a deceptive upward jerk, but this gets me nothing. The knot stays loosely off-center and the tie appears to be stuck somewhere underneath the collar at a point perhaps three inches to the right. After two minutes of this mad wrenching one of three things hap-

The tie refuses to budge.

pens—the tie rips, the collars tears, or I strangle to death in a horrid manner with eyes bulging and temples distended, a ghastly caricature of my real self.

Now this is a very strange thing to have happened in ten years. It can't be that I have forgotten how. It can't be that I have lost that amount of strength through loose living. It must be that some deliberate process has been adopted by the manufacturers to prevent four-in-hands from slipping under collars. What their idea can be is a mystery. You'd think they would *want* to make things as easy for their patrons as possible. But no! Modern business *efficiency*, I suppose! The manufacturers were *in conference*, I suppose! Rest-rooms for their women employees . . . oh, yes! Time clocks, charts, paper drinking-cups . . . oh, yes! But collars that hold ties immovable, and ties that stick in collars. That's what *we* get. That's what the Public gets. Prohibition was foisted on our boys while they were overseas, and while I was wearing soft collars the Powers-That-Be were putting the devil into stiff ones, so that when I come back to wearing them again I strangle myself to death. A fine civilization, I must say!

SIGNIFICANT RESULTS IN SECOND WEEK
OF OUR OWN STRAW VOTE

A S explained in a recent chapter (Vol. 92. No. 2398. *People vs. Luther Ferk*), we are working on a straw vote covering the entire nation, or at least some of it. This is done by a person-to-person canvass and vice versa, a system which results in the canvasser's meeting a lot of interesting people and making enemies of them. The author of this article (Robert Benchley) goes up to voters on the street or in bed or wherever they happen to be and asks them certain questions, all beginning with "W." Most of this was explained previously and if you didn't read the explanation you missed a very funny piece and it serves you right.

Following are the tabulations to date, with inferences to be drawn. Everyone must draw his own inference (on one side of the paper only) and any cheating will simply be laughed at.

RESULT OF STRAW VOTE TO DATE
(States shown covered with fur are normally Republican)

Interview No. 5. 41 years old. White male. Is against Hoover because he is a Negro.

Interview No. 6. 22 years old. White male. Mumbled so it was impossible to tell *what* he thought.

Interview No. 7. 45 years old. White female. Was at Lichy Lake all summer and didn't like it as well as last summer, owing to the McDostys' being there. The food was better than last summer but the crowd not so nice as a whole. Heard a good story the other day about a little boy who was asked by his teacher what a kangaroo was.

Interview No. 8. This included several people, all of whom got mixed up as the interview proceeded. One person would start to talk and then it seemed as if it were an entirely different person talking. This went on for some time.

Interview No. 14. (There were no interviews numbered 9, 10, 11, 12 and 13.) Is for Hoover because Hoover has been President for eight years and knows the ropes. To put a new man in would be folly. Besides, Smith is so mixed up with the Mohammedans that we would all have to be facing east every morning if he got in and this particular voter likes to face west.

RESULT OF STRAW VOTE TO DATE

Hoover	41	Hoover	41
Smith	41	Smith	41
Rogers	41	Rogers	41

(The above tabulation is all wrong)

In certain sections of the country it was found that there was a great deal of Rutherford B. Hayes sentiment, but purely sentiment, as Rutherford B. Hayes is not alive any more. (We shall probably get an indignant letter from Rutherford B. Hayes tomorrow, saying, "Like Mark Twain, the reports of my death have been greatly exaggerated.") It is hard to keep sentiment out of a political canvass, as people have their heroes and heroines (many still held to *Rowena* in "Ivanhoe" as their favorite heroine, but it has always seemed to us that *Rowena* was a little colorless. Give us somebody like *Becky Sharp*. Give us somebody like *Becky Sharp*, plenty of Charles Heidsieck 1919 and a cozy nook and watch the color come back into these cheeks!)

Later we may try to tell you about a big trend that we discovered—or rather, the trend that we *hope* to have discovered by then. We are on the trail of this trend now and hope to catch up with it any day if we hurry. When last seen, the trend had stopped over in Elkhart, Ill., to set its watch back an hour to Central Standard Time. Or would it be setting its watch *ahead?* We shall soon find out.

THE PACKER'S ASSISTANT

THERE is a great deal in the art of packing a suitcase or trunk. I might even let it go at that and go on to some other subject. However, having got you all excited about the art of packing, it would be rather mean of me to leave you flat.

At the risk of sounding methodical, I must advise making out a list of the things you want to pack before you even turn a hand to the actual work. In this way, you forget only those things which you forget to put down on the list, instead of the old way of forgetting things haphazardly. If you run over in your mind every article of clothing that you are going to wear on any particular occasion on your trip, beginning with underclothes and working right on up through and including overcoat, hat and even Inverness cape, you can hardly miss anything.

For example, suppose you are going hunting with a falcon. You stand very still with a pencil and paper, ready to jot down the items, and say to yourself (not loud enough to be heard, or they may not let you go), "Falconry shirt and running-pants— socks—old green sweater—kilt—dress-shoes—hood for falcon—falcon for hood—and derby." As you say each one of these, write it down on your list, and when you have finished you will have a neat little list, suitable for framing, and you will feel easy in your mind about not having forgotten anything, unless possibly the trousers. And with a kilt, you won't need trousers anyway—unless you are going to hunt after the sun goes down and it gets chilly.

Now all this should be done on the morning of your departure—provided you are departing late in the afternoon. This will leave you plenty of time to do the thing right and check up on your list. Of course, there will be some accessories which you will have to go out and buy, unless by some lucky chance you happen to live right in the back room of a men's furnishing store. People do, you know.

Let us say that, having made out your list, you find that you need some new studs and a tube of tooth-paste. One of the great natural phenomena is the way in which a tube of tooth-paste suddenly empties itself when it hears that you are planning a trip, so that when you come to pack it is just a twisted shell of its former self, with not even a cubic millimeter left to be squeezed out. You may think that you will buy it on the way to the train—in one of those drug-stores which clutter up the railway station when you are not traveling but which turn

One of the great natural phenomena is the way a tube of tooth paste suddenly empties itself when it hears you are planning a trip.

into fruit-stores and tobacco shops when you are
rushing for a train. My advice to you would be
to go right out and buy the tooth-paste the minute
you find you need it and don't start packing until
you have *everything* laid out on the bed.

Let us say that you discover that you need studs
and tooth-paste at eleven in the morning. Your
train leaves at five. (I'll bet you know right now
what train I'm thinking of.) You must go right out
then, *taking your list with you*, and go to the nearest drug-store, where you will also be wheedled into
buying a dictionary, having always needed one.

The studs, of course, will have to be bought at a
stud-store, and, as it will be very nearly lunch time,
it will be better to put off buying them until you
have eaten.

The choice of a place to eat when you are out
buying studs is very important and I would recommend a club of some sort if you happen to belong
to one. Here you will meet congenial people and
may perhaps even get into a bridge game. In that
event, it is well to remember that you lead the fourth
highest of your longest and strongest suit, and stick
to Scotch if you start out with Scotch. You can't
go wrong if you follow these directions to the letter.

If there is anybody in the club who can carry a
tenor, get him to come in and try humming "Ken-

tucky Babe." A good baritone would be too much to ask but there will be plenty who can fake a bass. And remember that when you come to the change, you slide from D to B to F *sharp* to E, and not from D to B to F *flat* to E, as so many novices at packing are likely to do. D, B, F *sharp*, E. That's right.

By now it will be quarter of five and all you have to do is to get home, throw a few things into your bag, *including your list* (so that you will know what to buy when you reach your destination), and you are off!

THE BIRTH OF A COLLEGE COMIC PAPER

SCENE: *The editorial sanctum of* THE RAZOR-BLADE, *the college comic publication, issued bi-weekly if the editors can get enough stuff together. It is* 9:30 *in the evening of the day on which all copy was due at the printers' at* 5.

EDITORS PRESENT: YOULING, '28, *Chairman;* BEAMISH, '28; ROFFEN, '29; PHIELO, '29. *The remaining twelve members of the Board have never been seen since their election in February.*

THE CHAIRMAN: Well, let's see, what have we got? What about the pictures?

PHIELO, '29: Do, do, yo-de-do, do-do-yo-de-do—

THE CHAIRMAN: Come on now! Cut the fooling! What pictures have we got?

ART EDITOR: Well, let's see, we've got four girls' heads and two full-lengths of girls lying on couches. Then there are four imitation John Helds and three straight he-and-she drawings with no jokes to go with them. And a caricature of—let's see, the name's on the back—a caricature of Dean Whiffy.

CHAIRMAN: What about text?

PHIELO, '29: Do, do-yo-de-do, do—

198

"There are four imitation *John Helds* and three straight he-
and-she drawings with no jokes to go with them."

CHAIRMAN: Come on now! Cut the fooling! We've got to get this number down tonight. What about text?

MANUSCRIPT EDITOR: Eighteen poems, five of them to Milady's ankle, and twenty-nine necking jokes. If we use them all, we are still five whole pages short.

CHAIRMAN: Well, let's see. Give us some pins. Give us a girl's head for the frontispiece and we can run the verse on skiing under it.

(ROFFEN *and* BEAMISH *leave, having ten-o'clock dates.*)

CHAIRMAN (*continuing*): Well, let's see. We can give each of the girls' heads a page. There's four full pages and four poems to go with them.

PHIELO, '29: Do you want any lemon peel in yours, Chief?

CHAIRMAN: Come on now! Cut the fooling! We've got to get this number down tonight. Give us some more necking jokes and find some drawings of two studes in fur coats to run over them. Put a John Held tracing on every other page. How many pages is that?

DUMMY EDITOR: We still lack three pages of filling.

CHAIRMAN: We'll have to run the best Held tracing as a full page and print one of the verses in

Old English type for a full page. Have we got one that sounds like Dorothy Parker's?

MANUSCRIPT EDITOR: Sure, they all do.

CHAIRMAN: Give us the best and get the printer to run a stock border around it. There's *that* page.

(ROFFEN *and* BEAMISH *return from ten-o'clock dates, accompanied by friends.*)

ROFFEN, BEAMISH AND FRIENDS: Sometimes I'm happy—sometimes I'm sad—sometimes I'm—

PHIELO, '29: Do-yo-do-de do, do yo do de-do, *Do!*

CHAIRMAN: Come on now! Cut the singing! We've got to get this number down tonight.

ROFFEN, BEAMISH AND FRIENDS, *joined by* PHIELO, '29: We've got to get the number down tonight, boys, we've got to get the number down tonight, was the trainman's lullaby.

CHAIRMAN: Oh, send what we've got down and mark "Copy to come" and "Space to fill" on the pages that don't fill.

THE ENTIRE BOARD, WITH FRIENDS (*exiting*): Do-do-yo-de-do, do-do-yo-de-do, Do!

A CHRISTMAS GARLAND OF BOOKS

AMONG the little bundle of books especially selected for Christmas-Wistmas, perhaps the most pat is "Rubber Hand Stamps and the Manipulation of India Rubber" by T. O'Conor Sloane. Into it Mr. Sloane has put the spirit of Yuletide which all of us must feel, whether we are cynical enough to deny it or not.

Beginning with a short, and very dirty, history of the sources of India Rubber, the author takes us by the hand and leads us into the fairy-land of rubber manipulation. And it is well that he does, for without his guidance we should have made an awful mess of the next rubber-stamp we tried to make. As he says on page 35: "It will be evident from the description to come that it is not advisable for anyone without considerable apparatus to attempt to clean and wash ("to sheet"), to masticate, or to mix india rubber." Even if we had the apparatus, we would probably be content with simply "sheeting" and mixing the india rubber and leave the masticating for other less pernickety people to go through with. We may be an old maid about such things, but it is too late now for us to learn to like new things.

It seems that in the making of rubber stamps a preparation knows as "flong" is necessary. Mr. Sloane assures us that anyone who has watched the stereotyping of a large daily newspaper knows what "flong" is. Perhaps our ignorance is due to the fact that we were on the editorial end of a daily newspaper and went down into the composing-room only when it was necessary to rescue some mistake we had made from the forms. At any rate, we didn't know what "flong" was and we don't want to know. A man must keep certain reticencies these days or he will just have no standards left at all.

It is not generally known how simple it is to make things out of rubber. "The writer has obtained excellent results from pieces of an old discarded bicycle tire. The great point is to apply a heavy pressure to the hot material. Many other articles can be thus produced extemporaneously." (Page 78.) This should lend quite a bit of excitement to the manipulation of india rubber. Imagine working along quietly making, let us say, rubber type and then finding that, extemporaneously, you had a rubber Negro doll or balloon on your hands! A man's whole life could be changed by such a fortuitous slip of the rubber.

Not the least of Mr. Sloane's contributions to popular knowledge is his sly insertion, under the very noses of the authorities, of what he calls the "Old Home Receipt" (ostensibly for "roller-composition," but we know better, eh, Mr. Sloane?). The "Old Home Receipt" specifies "Glue 2 lbs. soaked over night, to New Orleans molasses 1 gallon. Not durable, but excellent while it lasts." We feel sure that we have been served something made from this "Old Home receipt," but would suggest to Mr. Sloane that he try putting in just a dash of absinthe. It makes it more durable.

We can recommend Laurence Vail Coleman's "Manual for Small Museums" to all those who have received or are about to give small museums for Christmas. Having a small museum on your hands with no manual for it is no joke. It sometimes seems as if a small museum were more bother than a large one, but that is only when one is tired and cross.

From Mr. Coleman's remarkably comprehensive study of small museums, we find that, as is so often the case, income is a very serious problem. In financing special projects for the museum, such as the purchase of bird groups (if it is a museum that *wants* bird groups), there is a great play for ingenuity, and Dr. Abbott of the San Diego Museum of Natural History, tells of how they, in San Diego, met the problem:

The little cases containing bird-groups were offered to tradespeople in the city for display in their windows, the understanding being that the store should pay $50 for the advertising value. Thus, a meadowlark group, representing the male in very bright dress, the female, the nest and eggs, was paid for by a men's and women's clothing store and displayed in its window in the early spring with the slogan: "Take a pointer from the birds. Now is the time for your new spring clothes." A savings-bank took a woodpecker group, showing the storing away of acorns, and a California shrike group (Dr. Abbott ought to know) showing a rather sanguinary example of empaling surplus prey on the spines of a cactus, both displayed under the euphimistic caption "The Saving Instinct" and "Are You Providing for the Future by storing up your dollars [or cadavers] now?" A bush-tit's nest was taken by a real-estate firm and a mockingbird group by a music house. The local lodge of Elks gave $1200 for a case holding four elks (not members) and so, in time, the entire housing of the groups was accomplished and paid for. We are crazy to know what business houses paid for the rabbit and owl exhibits.

In the chapter on "Protection from Pests" we

looked for a way of dealing with the man in an alpaca coat who grabs your stick away from you as you enter the museum and the young people who use museums for necking assignations, but they were not specified. A blanket formula is given, however, which ought to cover their cases. "The surest way to get rid of pests is to fumigate with hydrocyanic acid in an airtight compartment, but this is a dangerous procedure which has resulted in a loss of human life. [Why "but"?] Another fumigant that is widely used is carbon bisulphide, but this is highly explosive and has caused serious accidents." This presents a new problem to museum-visitors and would seem to make the thing one of the major risks of modern civilization. If a person can't be safe from asphyxiation and mutilation while looking at bird-groups, where *is* one to be safe? It would almost be better to let the pests go for a while, at least until the museum gets started.

A collection of verse entitled "Through the Years with Mother," compiled by Eva M. Young, makes a nice gift which might perhaps be given to Father. It contains most of the little poems which have been written about mothers and the general tone of the thing is favorable to motherhood. One, entitled "A Bit O' Joy," wears off a little into child-propaganda, but probably would rank as a mother-poem too, for it is presumably the mother who speaks:

> Just a Bit-a-Feller,
>   Lips a bit o' rose,
> Puckered sort o' puzzled like,
>   Wonder if he knows—

There is one more verse explaining what the Bit-a-Feller might possibly know, but we didn't go into that. Another one which we left for reading on the train was entitled: "Muvvers" and begins:

> One time, I wuz so very small,
>   I prit' near wuzn't there at all—

We can not even tell you what the first two lines are of "Mama's Dirl."

The introduction to "Are Mediums Really Witches?" by John P. Touey begins by saying: "The sole purpose of this book, as its title suggests, is to prove the existence of a personal evil force and demon intervention in human affairs." This frightened us right at the start, for we are very susceptible to any argument which presupposes a tough break for ourself. There must be *some* explanation for what happens to us every time we stick our head out doors—or in doors, for that matter.

Mr. Touey begins with witchcraft in ancient times and comes right straight down to the present day. Even though he quoted "no less an authority than Porphyrius" in his earlier chapter, it was not until we got into the examples of modern people having their bed-clothes pulled off and their hats thrown at them that we began to feel uneasy. The story of the terrible time had by the Fox Sisters in Hydesville, N. Y., seemed pretty conclusive to us at the time of reading (2:15 A.M. this morning) and, frankly, we stopped there. And, believe it or not, a couple of hours later, during our troubled sleep, *some*thing pulled the bed-clothes out from the foot of *our* bed, and we awoke with a nasty head-cold.

We will pay $100 to Mr. Touey or Sir Oliver Lodge or anyone else who can help us locate the personal demon who has been assigned to us. We would just like to talk to him for five minutes, the big bully!

We can quote but one example of the fascinating problems presented in John A. Zangerle's "Principles of Real Estate Appraising" as we are limited in our space assignment, but perhaps from it the reader may get some idea of the charm of the book:

"Mr. Flanagan of New Zealand values this interest on the basis of an annuity using the 5%

interest tables.   Calculating the value on a 6%
basis he would proceed as follows: Lessor receives
$6,000 per annum for ten years, the present value
of which is 6,000 x 7.36 equals $44,160; plus the
present value of $12,000 per annum for 89 years
commencing ten years hence which is 12,000 x 9.254
(16.614—7.36) equals $111,048.   Lessor is also en-
titled to receive either possession or rent after 99
years have expired, the reversionary value of which
can be taken at $12,000 x 16.667 less 16.614 or .053
equals $636.   Thus $111,048 plus $44,160 equals
$155,844, the value of the lessor's interest."

How do you mean 16.614, Mr. Flanagan?   Aren't
you forgetting depreciation?

For those who like to browse along lazily with
British royalty, we can think of no less charming
way than to accompany Helen, Countess-Dowager
of Radnor through her 361-page book: "From a
Great-Grandmother's Armchair."   We had almost
decided not to begin it at all, until we read in the
Countess-Dowager's preface: "At the present time
I am resting 'on my oars' (or rather, in my Armchair) at my quiet country home, which, amongst
those of the third generation, goes by the name of
'Grannie's Peace-pool.' "   This gave us incentive to
read further.

And what a treat! "Grannie" certainly has earned her "peace-pool" after the exciting life she has led. Every year of her long career is given here in detail and it must make fascinating reading for the Radnors if only as a record of where the Countess left her umbrella that time in Godalming and who played zither in her "Ladies' String Band and Chorus" in 1879.

Among other things that are cleared up in this volume is the question of what the Countess did during those first hectic weeks of July, 1901.

"A good many engagements were crowded into the first fortnight of July," she writes modestly, "before going back to Venice. Among other things I passed a very pleasant week-end at Wendover Lodge with Alfred and Lizzie Gatty."

But the book does not dwell entirely in the past. Right up to the present day we have disclosures of equal importance. In September, 1920, while visiting in Bath, the following incident occurred:

"One Sunday I started off in the car to go and lunch with Mrs. Knatchbull. When we had gone a few miles, however, the car broke down, a 'rubber-washer' having perished and let the water through! We telephoned for a 'Taxi' which took me back to Bath, and the car was towed back. Later in the afternoon Mrs. Knatchbull sent a car for me to go over to tea, and I flew over hill and dale and reached her place in Babington in half an hour."

So you see, the Countess really *had* intended to lunch with Mrs. Knatchbull!

We neglected to mention that the authoress is by birth a Chaplin; so she probably can get free seats whenever Mary's boy Charlie comes to town in a picture.

THE WOOLEN MITTEN SITUATION

BEING A CONFIDENTIAL REPORT

This great historical document, sometimes referred to as the Epic of Advertising, is here presented, complete and unexpurgated, as delivered to the A. N. A. in Atlantic City.

I HAVE some very important data for all advertising men. I might as well admit right at the start that my first job on leaving college was with the advertising department of the Curtis Publishing Co. I am probably the only ex-Curtis advertising man who has not gone into the agency business for himself. As a matter of fact, when I left Curtis (I was given plenty of time to get my hat and coat) I was advised not to stick to advertising. They said that I was too tall, or something. I forget just what the reason was they gave.

But one of my last jobs before leaving Curtis was to go out on a commercial research trip for Mr. Charles Coolidge Parlin, the well-known Curtis commercial research sharp. Most of you have been

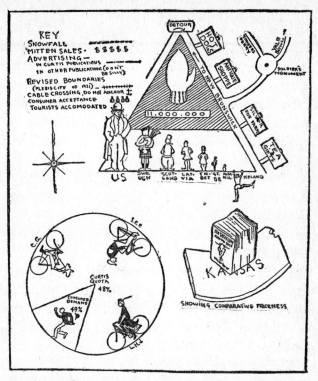

This chart shows something or other pretty graphically—we don't know just what except that Curtis is right, as usual. If the chart is correct there is certainly nothing like the Curtis Publications. At that you ought to have seen some of the dandy charts in Mr. Benchley's gingham report.

shown some of Mr. Parlin's reports—in strict con-
fidence—giving you the inside dope on the distribution of your own product and proving that, by using
exclusively the Curtis publications—their names
escape me at the moment—you will not only reach
all the public that you want to reach but will have
enough people left over to give an amateur performance of "Pinafore."

I used to have a hand in making up these Parlin
reports. My report on the gingham situation was
perhaps considered my most successful, owing to
the neat manner in which it was bound. It has been
estimated that my gingham report retarded by ten
years the entrance of the gingham manufacturers
into national advertising.

Looking through an old trunk last week I came
upon a report which I made for Mr. Parlin, but
which was never used. I would like to read it to
you tonight. It is a report on the woolen mitten
situation in the United States and was intended to
lead the way for a national campaign in the Curtis
publications to reach mitten consumers all over the
country.

In making this report I visited retail stores and
jobbers selling mittens in 49 states, asking the
following questions:

Of the retailers I asked:

1. Does the average woman, in buying mittens, ask for them by brand or just ask for mittens?

2. Does she try on the mittens for size?

3. Is there any appreciable consumer demand for mittens during the summer? If so what the hell for?

4. Is there any appreciable consumer demand for mittens during the winter?

5. Isn't it true that a mitten with a nationally advertised trade-name—like "Mitto" or "Paddies" —provided the Curtis publications were used exclusively—would sweep the field?

6. How many mitten buyers demand that the mittens be attached together with a string?

Of the jobbers we asked the following questions:

1. How do you like jobbing?

2. Are you a college man?

3. Wouldn't you be happier doing something else?

4. Do you ever, by any chance, sell any mittens?

Out of 4,846 jobbing establishments visited, only eight jobbers were found in. Jobbing establishments are always on such dark streets and there never seems to be anybody in the store. I finally got so that I would sit in my hotel and make up the jobbers' answers myself.

Now, as a result of this investigation, the Curtis

Company was able to place the following facts at the disposal of the various mitten manufacturers. Each mitten manufacturer was blindfolded and taken into a darkened room where he was made to promise that he would never tell any one the facts about his own business that he was about to be told. Then he was turned around and around until he was dizzy, and then hit over the head by the Curtis Advertising Director.

Following is the result of the mitten investigation:

1. In 49 states it was found that 615,000 women do not buy mittens at all. At first, these statistics would seem to be confusing. But, on being analyzed, it is found that 82 per cent. of these 615,000 women live in towns of a population of 50,000 or over, which means that they can keep their hands in their pockets and do not need mittens. Here, then, a consumer demand must be created.

2. From 5.6 per cent. to 95 per cent. of the department store sales of men's mittens are made to women. This just shows what we are coming to.

3. In the New England states one woman in ten buys ready-to-wear mittens instead of piece-goods from which to make her own mittens.

4. In the Middle West, one woman in eleven buys mitten piece-goods. This extra woman is accounted for by the fact that an aunt of mine went to live in Wisconsin last year.

In the South, they had never heard of mittens. At one place in Alabama we were told that they had drowned the last batch they had, thinking the inquiry had been for "kittens." This gave us an idea, and we made a supplementary report on kitten distribution. In this investigation it was found:

A. That there is no general consumer knowledge of breeds of kittens. In other words, a kitten is a kitten and that's all.

B. Four out of five kittens never do anything worthwhile in the world.

C. The market for kittens is practically negligible. In some states there are no dealers at all, and hardly any jobbers.

D. A solution of the kitten dealer-problem might lie in the introduction of dealer helps. In other words, improve the package so that the dealer can play it up. Give him a kitten he will be proud to display.

But to return to our mittens:

We have shown that a nationally advertised brand of mittens, *if* given the proper distribution and *if* adapted to the particular consumer demand in the different mitten localities throughout the country, ought to dominate the field.

We now come to the problem of the proper medium for such a campaign.

In the chart on this same page we have a pyramid representing the Curtis circulation. Eleven million people, of whom 25,000 are able to lift the paper high enough to read it. In this shaded section here is where the country club is going to be. This is all made land. . . . We come down here to a circle showing consumer demand, 49 per cent. . . . Curtis quota 48 per cent. and here is the State of Kansas which was admitted as a free state in 1856.

To continue: in 1902, the year of the war, there were 160,000 of these sold in Michigan alone. Bring this down to present-day values, with time and a half for overtime, and you will see what I mean. Of these, 50,000 were white, 4,600 were practically white and 4,000 were the same as those in Class A—white.

We have now pretty well lined up the channels of distribution for mittens and have seen that there is only one practical method for reaching the mitten consumer, namely, 52 pages a year in the *Post,* and 12 pages in color in the *Journal* and *Country Gentleman.* There will be no duplication here as the readers of the *Country Gentleman* go to bed so early.

In addition to the benefit derived from all this, the mitten manufacturers will be shown all over the Curtis building in Philadelphia and allowed to peek into Mr. Lorimer's office. And, if they don't like this plan for marketing their product, they can lump it, because it's all they are going to get.

This report was the start of the big campaign which put the Frivolity Mitten Co. where it is today. And, for submitting it, I was fired.

THE TYPICAL NEW YORKER

ONE of the most persistent convictions reported by foreign commentators on the United States (a group which evidently embraces all unoccupied literates of England and the more meditative sections of the Continent) is that the real America is represented by the Middle West. Aside from the not entirely adventitious question of who is to decide just what "the real America" is, there arises a fascinating speculation for breeders and students of climatic influence as to why a man living in Muncie, Indiana, should partake of a more essential integrity in being what he is than a man living in New York City. Why is the Middle Westerner the real American, and the New Yorker the product of some complicated inbreeding which renders him a sport (in the biological sense) and a man without a country?

Of course, at the bottom of it all is the generally accepted theory (not limited by any means to visiting scribes but a well-founded article in our national credo) that there is something about the Great Open Spaces which makes for inherent honesty and general nobility of character. Hence the firmly rooted superstition that a boy who has been raised on a farm is somehow finer and more genuine than a boy who has been raised in the city.

I remember once a mother whose three children were being brought up in the country (and very disagreeable and dishonest children they were, too) saying, with infinite pity of the children of a city acquaintance: "Just think, those kiddies have probably never seen a cow!" Just what sanctity or earnest of nobility was supposed to attach itself to the presence of a cow in a child's life I never could figure out, but there was an answer which might have been made that her own kiddies had never seen the Woolworth Building or the East River bridges at night. Among the major inquiries which will one day have to be made is one into the foundation for this belief that intimacy with cows, horses, and hens or the contemplation, day in and day out, of great stretches of crops exerts a purifying influence on the souls of those lucky enough to be subjected to it. Perhaps when the answer is found, it may help solve another of the pressing social problems of the day—that of Rural Delinquency.

However, so ingrained is this faith in the efficacy of live-stock and open spaces in the elevation of the race, that even to question it is to place oneself under suspicion of being a character who will bear watching by the authorities. So it will be perhaps just as well to pass quickly on to the second, and more specific, reason for our guest-writers' impression that the Middle West is America and that New York is just New York.

In most cases this is easily explained by following the New York itinerary of the guest-writer (and the word "guest" is used advisedly—it has been estimated that the total personal expenditures of visiting authors during their stay in America, if pooled, might possibly buy one American author one breakfast at the Savoy in London). The New York about which they write is the New York they have seen or have been told about by their hosts, and, for even the most conscientious among them, this cannot constitute more than a quarter of even the Borough of Manhattan.

Ford Madox Ford has even been so explicit as to call his recent book "New York Is Not America," and yet he admits in the course of his argument that, for him, "New York is intimately and solely the few miles . . . along Fifth Avenue and Broadway from the Battery." And, at that, Mr. Ford knows his New York much better than most foreigners who prescribe for it. The customary laboratory and field work entered into by New York diagnosticians from abroad consists of a luncheon at the Coffee House Club, visits to several of the more accessible night clubs, a peep into Greenwich Village, and a series of dinners more or less under the auspices of Otto H. Kahn. If they are really in earnest, they may be taken up into Harlem and shown the negro exhibit, or over to Long Island City and shown how Sunshine Biscuits are made. They ask questions of their dinner partners, and those answers which they cannot use in a "vignette" of New York they embody in a searching and comprehensive analysis of the American Woman. This is generally considered ample investigation on which to base a broad survey entitled "The Meaning of New York," or, as Mr. Ford has put it, "New York Is Not America."

For most visitors to Manhattan, both foreign and domestic, New York is the Shrine of the Good Time. This is only natural, for outsiders come to New York for the sole purpose of having a good time, and it is for their New York hosts to provide it. The visiting Englishman, or the visiting Californian, is convinced that New York City is made up of millions of gay pixies, flitting about constantly in a sophisticated manner in search of a new thrill. "I don't see how you stand it," they often say to the native New Yorker who has been sitting up past his bedtime for a week in an attempt to tire his guest out. "It's all right for a week or so, but give me the little old home town when it cames to *living*." And, under his breath, the New Yorker endorses the transfer and wonders himself how he stands it.

The New York pixie element is seen by visitors because the visitors go where the pixie element is to be found, having become, for the nonce, pixies themselves. If they happen to be authors in search of copy, they perhaps go slumming to those places where they have heard the Other Half lives. They don't want to be narrow about the thing. There are the East Side push-carts, which they must see and write a chapter about under the title of "The Melting Pot." Greenwich Village they have heard about, but that only fortifies their main thesis that New York is a gay, irresponsible nest of hedonists. Wall Street comes next, with its turmoil and tall buildings—rush-rush-rush-money-money-money! These ingredients, together with material gathered at the Coffee House Club and private dinners, and perhaps a short summary of the gang situation, all go into a word picture called "New York," and the author sails for home, giving out an interview at the pier in which he says that the city is pleasure-mad and its women are cold and beautiful.

Typical of the method by which the actualities of New York are taken by writers and translated into material for the New York of their dreams is the fantasy indulged in by Mr. Ford (in common, it must be admitted, with most of our domestic writers) of attributing the lights in the buildings along lower Manhattan to some province of fairyland.

"By day the soaring cliffs," writes Mr. Ford, "that rise joyously over behind the Battery are symbols not merely of hope but of attainment; after dark, and more particularly in the dusk, they are sheer fairyland. There is something particularly romantic in a Germanic sort of way about mountains illuminated from within . . . the million-wise illumination of New York is a lighter, gayer affair . . . the mind on seeing it connotes not subterranean picks and sweat but lighter more tenuous occupations—the pursuits of delicate, wayward beings."

Our visitors are confronted with so much gaiety in New York, especially where the lights are brightest, that they fall into the literary error of ascribing any metropolitan utilization of voltage to the pursuit of pleasure. And it *is* difficult to look at the lighted windows at the end of the island and not idealize them into some sort of manifestation of joy and exuberance. But if the writers who thrill so at the sight and translate it into terms of New York's light-heartedness could, by some sardonic and unkind force, be projected along any one of those million beams of fairy light, they would find that it came directly from an office peopled by tired Middle Westerners, New Englanders, and Southerners, each watching the clock as lighting-up time comes, not to start out on a round of merrymaking but to embark on a long subway ride up town. And this ride will take them on past the haunts that the visitors and their hosts know, past the clubs and theatres and squash-courts, to an enormous city above One Hundred and Twenty-Fifth Street, where life is, with the exception of a certain congestion in living-quarters, exactly the same as life in Muncie, Indiana, or Quincy, Illinois. For the inhabitants of this city have come direct from Muncie and Quincy and have never become assimilated into the New York of the commentators. It is not even picturesque, as the East Side is picturesque. It is a melting pot where the ingredients refuse to melt. The people are just as much New Yorkers as those in the Forties, and they outnumber the "typical" New Yorkers to so great an extent that an intramural battle between the two elements could not possibly last for more than twenty minutes, even if the pixies had machine guns.

I am not speaking of Harlem or the Bronx, where the standard of living is radically different from that of the much-advertised denizens of pleasure. Up in the Heights and beyond, as well as in the side streets farther down town, there are hundreds of thousands of men and women who go to bed at ten o'clock for the same reason that residents of Dodge City, Kansas, go to bed at ten o'clock—because they can't think of anything else to do, and because they have to be up at seven. There are streets north of Central Park through which a cooler breeze blows in summer than many a Mid-Western hamlet can boast, where life is quiet and its pace even. These streets are peopled by the very types who are supposed to make the Middle West the "real America," as alien to the New York of the magazine articles as their kinsfolk back home. They are in New York for many reasons, chiefly to make more money or because the head office in South Bend sent them there, and many of them wish that they had never come. But there they are, just as much New Yorkers as the patrons of Webster Hall or the Embassy Club, and a great deal more numerous.

I am not creating a New York out of my imagination as do those writers who find a filmy fairyland in the New York Edison Company's service along Pine and Nassau Streets. I have lived in New York's Middle West. During my early days as a

metropolitan rounder (fresh from Massachusetts)
I was under the wing of a kindly family from Can-
ton, Ohio, who lived in Washington Heights, and
it was a great comfort to me in my nostalgia to
feel that here, in this neighborhood, I was, to all

My first dissipation in New York was a church supper.

intents and purposes, among home folk.   My first
dissipation in New York was a church supper, so
identical with the church suppers I had known in
New England that it was impossible to imagine that
farther down on this same island was the gay
Gomorrah I had heard and been warned so much
about.   The people at this bacchanalia of chicken
salad and escalloped oysters matched to a man the

people I had eaten chicken salad and escalloped oysters with in my home town. There was the same aroma of coffee and hot rolls as one entered the vestry, and the same satyristic little boys were chasing the same coy little girls around the Sunday School room with as much vigor and obnoxiousness as if they had all been raised on a farm. Practically all of those present were small-town people, with small-town outlooks, and I venture to say that not one of them would have been recognized by a specialist in New Yorkese as a New Yorker. And yet there they were, they and their kind, a million strong.

Life in the New York Middle West goes along in its middle-class way with a dull rhythm which is in no way different from its model in Ohio or Michigan. Its pleasures are simple and inexpensive—movies, stock-company productions, church suppers, Masonic dances, and Sunday automobile riding in the country. When the day's work is done (and, as I understand it, even the real Americans in the Middle West have to attend to some sort of office work during the day aside from contemplating Nature in its more magnificent aspects) the same odor of cooking pervades the front halls, the same evening paper is read around the sitting-room table, the same problem of the evening's entertainment arises, ending in a general dozing in arm chairs and early retiring. Of sophistication there is none, of restlessness there is none (unless it be a restlessness to get back to Kansas or Massachusetts some day), and of the care-free fountain-fay that is the New Yorker of the correspondents you could go from one block to another all night long and not find a trace. There are simply dull, solid, one-hundred percent Americans, who have never been in a night club in their lives and have no desire to be in one, whose bridge game has barely progressed from the bid-whist stage, and whose evening clothes are still in the trunk in the cellar and couldn't be worn anyway.

Whatever mysterious qualities the Middle Westerner has which fit him for the rôle of "real American," his brother in New York possesses to an equal degree, although with perhaps not quite so much volubility. Just what the real America is supposed to be is a bit hard to define, for each commentator has a different idea. But almost all agree that the America of the Middle West is made up of bustling Babbitts, children of energy, forward-looking perhaps in politics but incurably chauvinistic and provincial in their world outlook. All of which might be a word picture of the rank and file of New York's great Region of Respectability.

For, when the final house-to-house analysis is made of New York, the Typical New Yorker will emerge as quite a disappointing and colorless figure. In a rather wavering and indefinite career in that city I have lived and worked in many sections. While trying to "find myself" (a search which I ultimately gave up) I have had jobs in Wall Street, the negro district of Harlem, the Tenderloin, and Park Row. At night I have gone home to Washington Heights, an East Side Settlement House, Greenwich Village, the roaring Forties, and Chelsea. About the only districts in which I have not, at one time or another, stayed are the wharf districts along the North and East Rivers, and certain sections of the Bronx and San Juan Hill. And, after fifteen years of this sort of thing, I still look a second time at the sight of a man in evening dress, waving toy balloons in a night club, and think: "Perhaps now I am seeing the New York life I have heard so much about." I still look a second time at a gunman, although I have given several their start in life in my boys' club days. And, although my present work—and play—takes me almost nightly into the slightly lopsided maelstrom of the pixie activities in the theatres and night clubs, I can never bring myself to feel that this can be the gay, lighthearted New York Life that produces the Typical New Yorker. It is all so Middle Western and tentative.

The New Yorker at whom one does not look a second time, because there are so many of him and, furthermore, because he would not justify a second look, is a composite of the small-town qualities of every State in the Union. He wears his soft felt hat in winter and his straw hat in summer and, when his day's work is done, reads the same things in the New York *Evening Sun* or *World* that he read in his home-town evening paper before he came to New York: the domestic news on the front page (nothing with a foreign date-line) and the sporting news. He has a vague feeling that he is not *au courant* with the world's events and thoughts, and so subscribes to *The Literary Digest* or *Times* —which his wife reads. He votes for Hoover because Smith is a Catholic, or for Smith because Hoover is an Anglophile, and feels much less strongly about the issue of Prohibition than the zealots on either side think. If anything touches his business interests, however, he is roused into action and becomes a Moving Force. He has two children and wants them to have a good education. He is one-hundred-percent American, one-hundred-percent business and one-hundred-percent dull. And much as he dislikes New York, he would live in no other place.

On a scale such as statisticians draw showing the comparative sizes of the standing armies of Europe, this man would tower over the small figures of the night-club rounder, the sophisticated *literatus,* the wage slave of the East Side, and the other popular conceptions of the New Yorker as the S. S. *Majestic* standing on end towers above a soldier in a Swiss uniform. He cannot be called a "typical New Yorker" because there is no such thing, but, if the man seen in the Middle West by the visiting writers is a "typical American," then this man is one too. Furthermore, he is the product of no one section of the country but of all sections.

All of which would seem to give New York a right to claim that within its boundaries alone can be found the real, composite America. But New York does not apparently care enough to make such a claim, which lack of civic pride and booster-spirit is perhaps the most un-American thing about New York.